Create
my
Happy

possibility, productivity & performance to #createmyhappy

The Three Ps

Possibility
Productivity
Performance

by Tabby Kerwin

First published by Mode for... Publishing in 2019.

Copyright © 2019 Tabby Kerwin with Mode for... Publishing.

www.modeforpublishing.com

For more information go to:

www.modefor.co.uk

www.facebook.com/modefor

www.facebook.com/modeforpublishing

www.facebook.com/createmyhappy

www.twitter.com/tabbykerwin

www.instagram.com/tabbykerwincreatemyhappy

www.instagram.com/modeforevents

INDEX

Foreword

When I started writing this book in the summer of 2018, I was sat with my laptop at the bedside of my husband, Simon, in St. James's University Hospital in Leeds. He had just started chemotherapy, having been diagnosed with cancer. Three months later, Simon was dead and my world was rocked. It was unexpected as he'd kicked the cancer. Life is cruel.

Fortunately for me, Simon had given me every skill I would need to get through and embrace grief into my life. He had supported me through my darkest of times over the previous decade and had given me the confidence to believe in myself and my abilities again. He was the one person who had made me happy and who had also taught me that it was OK to be happy whilst dealing with what life throws at you. He was my happy and always will be.

In 2018, I started my *#createmyhappy* revolution and began to refine what had helped me to get through the dark times, emotionally, physically and financially, whilst running and developing a business and being a wife and mum.

The Three Ps was born. I knew that there was always possibility, and that with productivity, you can perform the hell out of your life and business; and I wanted to share this with everyone. So, with Simon's support and gleeful eye and naughty jokes from his hospital bed, I started to write.

After a short hiatus as I dealt with funeral arrangements and adapting to life without Simon, I finished writing this book on the day that marked 100 days since his death. Today is not going to be a sad day. Today I'm celebrating putting in words all that this great man helped me to do and I'm promising him I will practise The Three Ps forever to be successful, creative and, most of all, happy.

Simon, this book is for you, my darling. Thank you for the love, the kindness, the support, the life, the friendship, the challenges, the business, the laughter, the music and, above all, for always making me *#createmyhappy*. I will love you forever.

1

Introduction

Hey! I'm Tabby and I shall be your guide through this little journey I like to call *#createmyhappy*.

I'm joining the happiness revolution not in a *happy-clappy, everything is wonderful* kind of way, rather a *let's all realise anything is possible for us, get our shit together, make a plan and implement it* kind of way.

There's a difference: one means you sit around hoping and praying for something to change in your life, whilst the other gives you the proverbial kick up the backside and reminds you you're in charge of your own life and you have to create your own success and happiness. This led me to calling the art of creating our own happiness *#createmyhappy*. Go on, hashtag the life out of it on social media!

These days we seem to get endless surveys, news reports and 'experts' telling us more people are suffering from anxiety and depression and struggling to be happy. The world seems such an overwhelming, competitive place at times, it's easy to understand why many people feel this way.

I know this: I've been there. Since my teenage years I have dealt with grief, anxiety and a fear of what others think; and whilst sometimes it has been a crippling battle to not let the demons take control of me, over time I've learned to keep the little buggers in check and with the implementation of my Three Ps plan, I'm always on a mission to *#createmyhappy*.

What are The Three Ps, I hear you say? Well, this book is wholly dedicated to them, and everything connected to them that will give you that push and get you back on track. They are three of my favourite words: possibility, productivity and performance.

Without these, there is no hope, no plan and no show – the three elements our lives are made up of. So, are you ready for the ride? Ready to get some perspective, make a plan and begin implementing it? I'll be your host and will be with you every step of the way. I'll show you what I've learned, how to get your mindset right, how to make plans, give you exercises to try – and we'll get a fabulous performance from you, to make you the happiest, best version of yourself.

I'll be kind along the way, let you into secrets and share personal experiences, but don't be under any illusions that once you've read this book (or any other similar book on Amazon or in the bookshops) everything will be magically fixed, because it really won't be. The only way you're going to make a difference in your own life is by taking action on what you believe and by taking control of your own life, success and happiness.

Without further ado, let's crack on. Let's get firing on all cylinders and show you how to *#createmyhappy*. Ready? Let's go.

2

About Me

What can I tell you about me that you can't already Google or find out elsewhere? Well, the public persona of me (in no particular order) is this:

Tabby Kerwin: events specialist, wedding fixer, professional musician, performance coach, writer, speaker and educator, business owner, mum, wife, widow and friend.

I guess what you really need to know is what qualifies me to write a book about being happy. Well, that's simple. I spent so much of my life not being truly happy, dealing with grief, demons, a failed marriage, being a mum and other people's opinions of me, that I was kept in a pretty low place – until the day I realised the key to happiness is in my own hands and other people's opinions are not my concern. That's what qualifies me: experience and honesty.

I still have to deal with all those issues, but now I know that by combining possibility and productivity, I can put on a great performance and *#createmyhappy*. Don't get me wrong, life throws you curveballs, and I still have occasional down moments in my days. The difference, though, is that I know how to ride the waves now – and that's a game changer.

3

My Why

My Why is to inspire, create and communicate. I'm a doer. I like to fix things and create happiness to make life easier for others, even if this is sometimes to my own detriment. That's why I've written this book: to help you fix things in your life and business so you can create your happy.

My message and values are not complicated. There's nothing in this book that will overwhelm you. It's just common sense (granted that's not always as common as it should be!) and everything is based on my personal story and experiences. I'm not a qualified counsellor or an expert on mental health and people, but I have a story and want to share it to inspire, motivate and educate.

Treat this book as your guide to simplifying the thoughts in your head – a permission slip to open your mind and believe that anything is possible – and then, together, we're going to create a plan which is productive and effective so you can go on to give your best performances.

As cheesy as the quote may be, I want to *live, laugh and love*. Even if I haven't always done this myself, I do now and I wish that for you, too. I want you to create the life you dream of because, do you know what, that dream can be a reality with the right mindset and action plan. But it's not just thoughts that will get you there, you have to take action.

Enough about me. I'll reveal more honest stories, memories and anecdotes throughout the book and hopefully, from my life experiences, mistakes and wins, you will be inspired to become the best and most successful version of yourself – and that's exciting. I'm excited. The change is going to be incredible and if you're up for it, this could be the start of a really stimulating journey to success. Most importantly, you're going to *#createmyhappy*.

First things first. Now you've committed, the first thing you need to be open to is learning; so, let's go and learn some amazing things that will open our minds and set us up for our incredible journey.

4

My Story

My journey has been full of twists and turns: the death of my father from cancer as a teenager, studying as a professional musician at one of the UK's leading conservatoires, struggling with my own personal demons and hitting an all-time low due to the actions of others. I have divorced, single parented, experienced the joy of finding love with Simon and getting re-married, been a carer for Simon, who was diagnosed with cancer in July 2018, and gone full circle back to grief when he died in November of the same year; all the time whilst running my own business, working hard developing my career and being a mum. But, despite what life has thrown at me, and losing everything, I have gained so much. It has taken time, but I have accumulated knowledge, experience, self-understanding, ambition, a successful business, an incredible son, a flexible lifestyle, friendships I love, and happiness; and so can you.

The Early Years

My childhood was fantastic and I look back on it with the fondest and loving of memories. It was steeped in music and horses, in idyllic surroundings, and I went to a prep school you could only dream of these days, Sibton Park. At 13 years old, I headed to one of the most highly respected all-girls boarding schools, Benenden; not because my family were rich but because we all worked hard together to secure bursaries and funding. I was awarded a music scholarship, thanks to the unwavering encouragement and mentoring of my father, who was a professional musician of the highest calibre and Head of Music at Sibton Park.

To be honest, my dad was a total legend and everyone that knew him loved him, from the children he taught to the friends he worked and socialised with and more beyond. He was my world: I was such a daddy's girl. So, in 1994, when I was 16 years old and he was cruelly taken away from us after an 18-month battle with cancer, my world was completely shattered. I had lost the most important person in the world to me and life would never be the same again. Now, this is a time when any 16-year-old should be allowed to grieve and cry, be angry or sad, lost or hurt – and be guided – but this is where both the best and worst of my life skills kicked in.

The evening my father died I was meant to be heading back to boarding school for the start of the summer term, and I remember clearly the phone call I made to my then housemistress, Mrs. Brinkhurst (or 'Brinky', as she was affectionately known), saying I would not be returning and the reason why. I was calm, relaxed and stress-free, just dealing with things strategically, unemotionally and professionally. Not what you expect from a 16-year-old girl who has just lost her daddy, but this was the start of me 'just dealing with things', whilst everyone else around me was losing the plot! (Just a side note: everyone at the school was fantastic and understanding, but as I reflect some 25 years later, I realise there was nothing in the way of support or counselling. Certainly nothing like what my son has been offered since the death of Simon.)

Whilst family and friends grieved and dealt with it with a mixture of sadness, loss, blame, denial and, in hindsight, some through downright selfishness, I was pretty much left to work everything out for myself (not by my mum I must add; she was a rock star who had had her own world shaken beyond belief).

From funeral planning to competing in music competitions five days after he died to returning to school a few days later to commence my GCSEs, there was no time to grieve; and then there was the next thing I had to do, or fix, or be strong for and so it continued. I put my own emotions to the back of the queue and made sure everyone else was OK and everything else that needed doing got done. This was to become a theme in my life, and a lot of those historical emotions are still at the back of the queue in my mind, *but they are content.*

The Late Teens

So, let's skip on a few years. I did very well in my GCSEs, spent two years studying at the Junior Guildhall School of Music & Drama on Saturdays (the last thing my dad saw me successfully audition for) whilst remaining at boarding school to take my A Levels – which I nailed – and then headed north to Manchester to study at the Royal Northern College of Music. (I'm glossing over the getting in trouble at school for drinking champagne and a few other shenanigans along the way. They were all just character-building misdemeanours done with style!)

As a young girl, my life was planned out to study music in London, and as my mother always reminds me, 'You wouldn't have gone to Manchester if your father was alive.' Yet, this move was my decision. (Side note: I probably would have still gone to Manchester if my father was alive because, at the end of the day, he always supported what was right for me and my happiness.) I was going to where my friends and my best support network were and this was the start of my time and my adult life. So, in early September 1996, I packed up my little white Nissan Micra, which looked like a roller skate, and headed to Manchester, pretty much never to return to Kent aside from fleeting visits to see family. I needed to escape and even today I need to keep the Kent countryside at a distance.

University life was everything I knew it would be; but, for me, it was a different adventure from your average student's. I wasn't a kid who had never left home until then. I was the one that had been in boarding school for five years, lost my dad and supported everyone else – I'd lost my childhood years ago, so being an adult was not unusual to me. I lived with my best friends, I earned money whilst I studied and I organised other people in bands, music groups and other social circles to make sure they got the life adventures they craved. This was usually to my own detriment as I was either the duty driver or the person that sacrificed their own free time – and life – into the bargain.

Adulting: The Good and The Bad (and The Ugly)

In my penultimate year of university, I met the man that was to be my first husband. In 2002, we were married; in 2004, my gorgeous son Oliver was born. I had been working as a freelance musician, music journalist and PR person since before I graduated. (My graduating is a bone of contention. My tutor tried to fail me on my degree because I had the balls to do what I wanted as a career and not be bullied by an institution. Learn a lesson from this: always do what you believe is right for you.) I was also playing principal cornet and managing a brass band in Yorkshire. This sounds like a small, insignificant job, but I cannot begin to tell you the number of hours that go into such a voluntary job. It's all-consuming, more time than a full-time job and you receive very little, if any, thanks whatsoever, from anyone. It's always on you when people don't get what they want personally, yet they do little to assist.

I was living in a world of trying to balance and juggle every ball, plate, knife and flamethrower lobbed at me and managing it as best as anyone could, yet the people that had one ball to throw in two hands, with someone to help them, were the critical ones, who obviously could do everything better. You know the type: lots to say but take very little action.

In 2008, Simon and I set up Mode for…. It started as a music publishing business, with a brass teaching book which Simon wrote and I edited, but it wasn't long before it started to develop organically. With our experience as musicians and event organisers, we let the business take its natural path, based on an ethos of doing what we love and having fun: supplying musicians, managing events and more. I finished much of my freelance writing work to concentrate on the business and it was a great learning curve. I'd always loved the flexibility of a freelance work lifestyle and having control was great because you could learn so much every day.

Cut forward a few years and things started to go wrong – badly wrong – anything that could go wrong did. 2010 was the all-time low: I couldn't cope and all I wanted was a way out. It was a way out of life that I wanted; I just wanted to make everything go away permanently. It was probably clear to someone that I was struggling in my own head, but no one said anything. I say that but I hid everything from my best friends and family and everyone else in my life did not care enough about me to see anything was wrong. They were too busy concentrating on getting what they wanted and blaming everyone else for everything and anything (remember the type of people I described before!).

I was miserable, utterly miserable, but it was more than 'feeling down'. It was deeper. The type of feeling that makes you believe you can't physically function, that everything is a mess and the smallest of activities is the biggest effort. But what did I do? Did I seek help at that time or talk to the people in my life about it? No, of course not. What was the point? In my mind, they weren't really interested in me after all. So, I did the same as I did when I was 16 years old and bottling up my grief: the performer came out in me. I sucked it all up and got on with things. But I hated every day. I would lie in bed with a feeling of dread and fall asleep hoping the morning wouldn't come. From the outside, all seemed normal; but on the inside, I had lost myself. Then I had my moment of clarity, on the A64 east of York at 10.30pm on a Thursday night – on my own with a puncture.

I had two choices, but I had a little boy at home and I knew I had to make life better for us. I had to fix me because no one else ever had or would. There had to be a better and happier life.

It was going to be a long, hard road (metaphorically and literally, with one of those space-saving tyres you can't go above 50mph on!), but it was a journey I had to take. So there it began.

The one thing I did accept first was that it was going to get a lot worse before it got better. The people I gave so much for were clearly just not compatible with my life; whilst I gave them everything, the majority gave nothing in return. My marriage finally ended in April 2011. I left behind what seemed like everything except my son, my business and my three best friends. I took myself out of the environment of the people who were not compatible with me, those whom I couldn't do right by no matter what I did for them. I was even more wrong when I took myself out of their lives. But what's that phrase? 'The haters are going to hate.' You bet they do, for a long, long time and a bit longer still.

I could document every bit of my life through this God-awful time but do you know what, there is no point. I don't want to hash up every bad feeling I felt due to the actions of others in real time. I live with them every day and have clarity on them now. The reality is that I hit rock bottom, bottled it up and started my own journey to finding a way out of the tunnel. As I was making my journey out, everyone around still chose to try and stop me, mainly because they were too blind to see what I was really feeling because I was always the strong one. But I kept on going with that 'snow shovel' and life in front of me.

I was continually affected inside by everything every person said. My external strength was constantly misconstrued as not being caring or as being selfish, but the reality was so far removed from this. I had to work out what to do. So, with head down, I concentrated on letting the business take its natural developmental course and I removed myself from the people and worlds I'd once frequented. I knew they were poisonous to me and I began to learn that what they thought was not up to me.

Simon was fantastic as a support and my best friend at this time, and that's why I eventually chose to make my life with him. Marrying him was the best decision I made after setting up a business with him. We were truly compatible and we developed new friendships with people who are simply fabulous. Slowly over the years, I have carefully selected the right people to be in my life. I have the most fantastic friends who I'd do anything for, and unlike previous people in my life, I know these friends would do anything for me – and they do.

From Then to Now

I want to jump to the present day now, to shift the focus on how I managed to figure everything out in my own head. It has taken me several years to get there – actually, nearer a decade. And yet, despite the business flourishing beyond belief, Oliver becoming an amazing young man, spending time in our home in Umbria and marrying the most fantastic man, there were times when it was still a relentless battle. The death of my brother in 2014 following a long battle with depression and the recent devastation of my darling husband Simon's cancer diagnosis, followed by his death from treatment-related complications in November 2018, have given way to new struggles.

Yet, I've learned some major things, such as that it is essential you work and socialise with people that are compatible and leave anyone else behind. I've learned it's OK to be selfish and seek what you want (because that isn't actually selfish); and I've learned that it is OK not to be OK but, equally, it's OK to be great. Having the right people around you means you can share with them, you don't always have to be strong. We are emotional beings and we must focus, embrace and challenge our own personal emotions both with and in spite of other people. Look after yourself first and that will make you stronger for others. I've also learned that in the last decade, my life has developed immeasurably; yet, the negative people in my life from times gone by seem to be stuck in the same place, saying the same things, just about somebody different (and occasionally still me!).

The biggest thing I have come to realise is that everything I've been through and am currently going through has been a lesson: it's made me stronger, it's made me better and it's enabled me to help you avoid going through the same things in the same way. Through learning and strategies, confidence, performance, discipline and inspiration, I now create my own flexible life that I love – and I'm here to help you do the same. Whether you want to launch your own business, re-design your existing life or business or just want to get your creative or personal mojo back, I'm here to help and support you. Every day presents us with a combination of success, pressures and challenges, but by celebrating everything good along the way, you will be able to methodically ride out the challenges.

Wow! That is about as honest as it gets (minus a few names and details), but you can see that I've got the experience in life and business to help you be stronger.

#createmyhappy

I started the *#createmyhappy* 'revolution', if you like, in 2018. It was my eureka moment when I truly realised and believed that we each have the choice to be happy, regardless of what we are going through or experiencing in life; and that's the thing, we are in charge of our own emotions.

You see, so often it's easy to REACT to things as opposed to ACT. We let our overall mood dictate what and how we do things. When we're in a good mood it's great: we're happy and everything we do is with a spring in our step. Yet when our overall mood is bad and we are down, angry or sad we struggle to see or do anything other than respond under the veil of that mood. This is where my *#createmyhappy* comes into its element. It's the realisation that despite your overall mood you have the choice to be happy and not just react to everything in a negative way.

We choose our emotions. No one *makes* you angry – you decide to use anger as a response to a situation. Agreed? So, why not choose happy and decide to bring happiness into your life despite what might be going on around you.

Often, we put ourselves in situations where we resort to habitual reactions. Let's take, for example, the self-scan machine at the supermarket! I was stood at one of these, minding my own business, while a man next to me was getting very frustrated and angry at the machine because it kept requiring store personnel verification for every item. He was getting increasingly wound up and said, 'This machine does this to me every time. It always makes me mad and I was already having a bad day.'

But you see, the machine didn't make him mad. He chose to react like that to something he knew was likely to happen. He could have chosen to act totally different – positively – and this would have changed his emotions, but instead he was dictated by his overall mood. Choosing to act differently towards the situation would have had totally different consequences, resulting in him having a better day.

How often do you let an event, person or feeling dictate your mood?

If something great happens, how is your mood? How do you behave?

If something sad, annoying or devastating happens, how is your mood? How do you behave?

Think of a time when something really great happened and how that affected you. Likewise, think of a time when something really bad happened and how that affected you. Did you let your overall mood affect how you responded to things or did you consciously choose how to respond? Do you think that the situations could have benefitted from choosing to be happy? What could you have changed?

5

Be Prepared to Learn

I love learning. I love constantly developing myself personally and professionally and learning about useful things, as well as random things that I may never use again.

This wasn't necessarily the case whilst I was at school, though. I'm definitely one of those people that now wishes they'd treasured and appreciated their learning during the school years a little more and maybe put in more effort. That's not to say I didn't learn loads. I can still vividly remember lessons and teachers from over 30 years ago and can recall random facts. I clearly learned more at the time than I thought and it's only now, in my 40s, I'm actually using some of this information!

I think it's a shame people think you stop learning when you finish formal education. For me, this is when learning truly begins. It's a time when you're not restricted to only learning about certain subjects for exams or assessments. The world becomes a completely open book and you can choose what page you read. What's more, it's the time when you really start getting to know yourself. This is when the adventure begins.

These days, my learning mainly comes from reading, writing, talking and travelling, four things I love to do. I love different cultures and their arts, food, wine, history and people, and languages especially. You can learn so much from communicating with people; a simple conversation with a stranger can open so many doors, and drinking in the knowledge of others can be totally intoxicating.

I find it a shame so many people lock themselves away in an office or behind a computer and never take the opportunity to interact, socialise and communicate or to experience the wealth of knowledge all around them. This can often lead to anxieties about mixing with other people.

Learning is the key to so many things and it certainly opens your eyes to all the possibilities that surround you. Learning can inspire you, excite you and free you. It can drive you to try something new which may be the thing that creates your happiness or success and if you hadn't have opened yourself up to the possibility of learning that something new, you would have never found out.

Experiences: we all need to experience things to develop. We need to dive in and get our feet wet and hands mucky in the pool of knowledge. We need to live and learn, love and laugh as we do it. We need to visit places and people and be hungry for more.

Most importantly, we need to fail and make mistakes because this is when we truly learn. I am a huge believer that we only succeed from getting things wrong. In doing so, we can develop and grow and try something different to make ourselves even happier, more successful and stronger.

What was the last thing that you learned? What, where or who gave you this lesson?

6

Create My Happy

Now it's time to get to the crux of *#createmyhappy*. It's simple: it's about balancing everything you have going on in life and work with creating your own happiness to maximise success and freedom.

If you take control and create your own happiness, without relying on anyone or anything else to make you happy, you will most definitely open yourself up to great possibilities, be super-productive and give the best performances of your life.

Ready to *#createmyhappy* – let's crack on and make it happen then.

i. Happiness

What is happiness? For starters, happiness is a choice. Even during the toughest of times, we can choose to be happy. You can be sad and still experience happy thoughts and events. Happiness can be balanced with other emotions, but it is down to you to choose it.

Let's break happiness down a little into this simple equation:

Happiness = wellbeing + wealth + honesty

I say wellbeing instead of health because even during illness it's possible to look after your mind and wellbeing. I say wealth because there is a difference between wealthy and rich and wealth is not dependent on money. I say honesty because everything starts with you being honest with yourself. But I will come back to all these points later.

Why do you want to be happy? Is it because you're tired of feeling down and negative or maybe it's because you look at people around you and think they are happier? The truth of people that are genuinely happy is that they have chosen to be that way – they have made a conscious decision to live each day in a happy way.

For me, I make my choice to be happy because I've realised and experienced the benefits of that mindset; and that's all it is, a mindset. If I wake up and don't make those conscious decisions to be grateful and happy, my day will be unproductive, messy and make me feel down. But if I exercise my power of choice and consciously decide to find the good in each day, starting with first thing in the morning, then I will start my day with a great mindset. I will know things are possible and the day will be rewarding.

So, what stops us? Why do we block our own happiness and sabotage our own lives? Mainly because our default is to not exercise this skill and to let ourselves be overwhelmed by everything going on in our lives.

Why not start your day with a little gratitude? Simply waking up, being alive and able to live another day is reason enough to be thankful and to celebrate. First thing each day, think about what possibilities lie ahead, not what overwhelms you. Train your brain to think in a more positive way. Adjust your mindset to be grateful for what you do have and what you could achieve, before worrying about what you don't have or can't do.

This simple conscious decision could be the starting point of a whole new mindset for you, the one small step that will open you up to inviting more happiness and freedom into your life and the key to a whole new way of living. Stop sabotaging your own happiness and make a choice: a choice to be happy.

ii. Wellbeing

Originally, I had this chapter entitled *Health* but I think *Wellbeing* is better since I've come to learn that sometimes illness and bad health is out of our hands, with so many cruel diseases taking hold of the fittest and healthiest people, as cancer did with Simon. Wellbeing, however, is something within our own control.

Good health and wellbeing are vital to your life and a major player in the mission to *#createmyhappy*, but wellbeing is your priority. If you don't look after yourself first, you cannot begin to look after anyone else or achieve the things you want to achieve. Yourself, your family, your friends and your work need you in top shape, so invest in yourself.

When we talk about health and wellbeing we automatically think about physical health, probably followed by diet (another word I'm not sure it is good to focus on nutrition is far better), but we should be focussing on our mental wellbeing first.

If we can be honest, disciplined and kind to our mind, it will follow that we will be kinder and more supportive of our own physical wellbeing. It is important to free your mind enough to have clarity; this clarity will in turn lead you to experience the feeling of possibility, and that is the route we are looking to take.

But how can we be kind to ourselves and our minds? Firstly, stop comparing yourself to others, whether that is physically or in work, family or any other way in which you measure yourself against what you see in magazines, on TV or on your social media feed. Remember that what you are seeing and trying to compare yourself to is just the edited highlights that have been selected for you to view, not the reality. Focus on your own life, achievements and goals and your mind will instantly feel a lot more at peace.

Allow yourself to embrace all your emotions whether good or bad. Don't try to fight negative emotions or issues; instead, accept them, learn from them and turn them into an experience or opportunity to develop.

I'll cover much of these areas later, but for now, fill your life with exercise and nutritious food and remember that anything eaten in moderation is good. Don't feel you have to be a slave to a gym if that's not what you enjoy. Go for a walk and be inspired by the nature around you; it's a fabulous way to exercise and what's better you can go with a friend and chat, grab a great audiobook or just walk in silence, being mindful and appreciative of everything around you. I love walking and yoga as my go-to relaxing and inspiration exercise regimes. I sometimes run, but usually under duress or because I have set myself another challenge like running a marathon. I don't actually enjoy running at all, but I do love the feeling of nailing a challenge!

Food-wise, don't bully yourself about sticking to regime and diets. You're a clever person (you must be, you're reading this book!), so be kind to yourself and eat mindfully. Eat foods that are natural and nutritious and eat enough of the good stuff in sensible portions and don't deprive yourself of treats. Deprivation never works and makes our minds sad. We want to *#createmyhappy*. Listen, I'm no food or exercise expert, but I'm sure we all know what's good and bad. If you don't, go get some great advice from the people that really know their stuff. Remember to drink lots of water. Dehydration is not only bad for you, it dampens your creativity and spirit.

Want to know another great way to look after your mind and ensure fabulous wellbeing? Do what you love and love what you do. Simples! Whether that's for work or pleasure, filling your life with what and who you love is an amazing way to feel great, so get back into those hobbies and things for you. They come first! You come first: never forget that.

iii. Wealth

I class myself as wealthy. No, I'm not bragging about having endless pots of money and being rich as hell as I don't and I'm not, but I am very wealthy.

Don't get me wrong, money is great and essential to pay the bills and get through life. I've been to the lowest point of financial struggle, with debts and making ends meet. When you walk round the supermarket with a list of meals mapped out and a calculator counting every last penny; when you dread the postman arriving as it's another demand; when you fear the scary collections man turning up on your doorstep so you never open the curtains and keep the door locked: I've been there. It's horrendous. But I've moved on from that to a place of balance and wealth.

I'll explain. I personally don't believe that being rich and being wealthy are the same thing and I don't believe you have to be rich to be happy. In fact, many rich people aren't truly happy. My ideal now is to earn enough money for everything I need to pay in bills and lifestyle, plus a little extra for things I love, like books, experiences and travel, and to balance this with a deep gratitude and appreciation for everything I have that makes my life wealthy.

The things that have made me wealthy are my fabulous, loving husband, who taught me to smile again; my son; and having the flexibility to do what I want each day with my work and career, choosing how I work so I can love what I do and do what I love. Spending time with the people I love, reading, relaxing at home, making people happy by helping and supporting them, grabbing a cheap flight and spending time in Italy, writing, cooking, listening, music and experiencing new things in life: all these things, so many of which cost nothing, make me wealthy. I now focus on experiences and people and not things.

In 2011, my ex-husband and I split up. I knew I could be happier in my life and bravely addressed the issues. I moved out of our £250,000, five-bedroom house into a small two-bedroom rented cottage in the same village with my then seven-year-old son. In the UK, we are obsessed with buying houses, having mortgages and moving up the housing ladder to the absolute best we can just about afford (whilst struggling with mortgage payments and sacrificing living for material assets), so to many people, this seemed like a lot to leave behind.

Maybe it was, but I wasn't concerned with the value of bricks and mortar and living in the 'big house' to keep up with other people. I needed to escape that marriage and life, breathe again, be free and find happiness, even though I knew it wouldn't be easy at first.

As I sit here writing this book now, some eight years later, I am still living in that very same rented two-bedroom cottage, which I have shared over the years with my son, fabulous husband and cats! We've grown and lost as a family. We have our business, and are at home a lot between trips and events, and whilst we often considered moving into a much bigger house, we didn't. Why? It's simple: this small, beautiful cottage is home. I don't care that I don't own it and it's rented – there's no real stigma with that. When I was young, I would imagine my ideal home and it would be an old cottage with mullion windows, a huge fireplace, an Aga and original beams. I live in my dream home; I just didn't realise it for a while, but now I do and I appreciate how wealthy I really am.

Living here allowed us to buy a property in a beautiful Italian town on the edge of a lake, which is our happy place and one we adore. It's peaceful and blissful and idyllic. When I tell people we have a home in Italy they think we must be incredibly rich to buy overseas, but the reality is it didn't take being rich. It took a desire to do something, working out whether it was possible and coming up with a plan to grab what we wanted, which we did in 2012.

Yes, it is the most amazing place I've been to and somewhere I am truly happy, but the house itself is a houseboat, moored in a sailing club, it looks like a shed, and is a floating studio apartment within said shed that floats and goes nowhere (except the once in high winds when it escaped! Whoops!). It cost us £11,000 to buy outright and we pay an annual fee to the sailing club of about £1,000, a 'ground' rent if you will, for it to be there and that includes utilities. We can grab a cheap flight for around £50 and be there in a few hours.

What we have is the most precious thing, one which I'm so grateful for. It has offered us the opportunity for so many memories, but it cost a fraction of the amount you'd normally spend on buying a house or even on a holiday for some people. So, I have my ideal home in both the UK and in Italy. I am incredibly wealthy and fortunate, but it didn't take a bucketful of cash.

There are so many ways in which you can consider yourself wealthy. Eating incredible food, for example, can really enrich your life – and at an affordable cost. By grabbing great-priced ingredients and learning to cook yourself, you can cut down on how much it costs to experience these meals. It doesn't take money to be wealthy, it takes contentment in everything you have, plus a vision of possibility, a great plan and then going for it.

How wealthy are you? List down everything in your life that makes you wealthy.

iv. Honesty

Let's get something clear from the outset about honesty. I'm not saying you have to reveal all of your secrets and share absolutely everything. Far from it. We all have, and I think *should* have, secrets. Secrets can often give us a sense of excitement or protect others from hurt. Things happen, secrets happen, don't worry about it. Like your other emotions, embrace them.

I'm not interested in secrets but in you being honest with yourself and others about what you want, need and desire, and your successes and shortcomings. You need to be honest with yourself before you can be honest with others, though, and this honesty will help you respect yourself. This may be personal or work-related honesty.

I was honest with myself when I knew I could be happier in my life. That honesty opened my eyes to possibilities, made me have courage and, consequently, led to freedom out of my last marriage. I went on to gain an amazing sense of freedom, combined with love and support from Simon, who I was then blessed to call my husband.

Could you do with being fitter so you can enjoy more fun with your family?

Could you achieve more success in your business if you brought in more skilled people to do certain tasks?

Would employing someone to do the cleaning just an hour a week not only free you up some time to focus on you but also give you a cleaner house?

Would that check-up at the dentist actually make you feel better as you won't continue to feel anxious about going?

Would launching that product, book or service you've been thinking about, but been too scared to do, actually bring you in an extra stream of income you need?

Whatever your question to yourself, be honest about the answer. We don't have to be great at everything and we don't have to fear things we don't know the answer to. Honesty can open your eyes to a whole lot more possibilities, which in turn leads to happiness.

Often, we fail to be honest with ourselves or others because we are scared of what they will think or say. My response to that these days is courtesy of the words of a very wise friend who is sadly no longer with us: 'Other people's opinions are not your concern.'

I have been guilty of being so overwhelmed by the opinions of others in the past and that anxiety has led me to some very dark places; however, the amazing thing I have learned over time, as a direct result of being honest with myself and taking on board what people have said to see if there is any truth in it, is that their opinions truly mean nothing because my life has changed, progressed and developed so much for the better. As I have already said, all those people are still doing the same thing, in the same place, with the same people and are still unhappy and commenting on others.

To those people that made me feel so bad and anxious and tried to destroy me, I thank you. Your attempt at destruction to make yourselves feel better has driven me to incredible, happy things.

v. It's OK to Not Be OK … But, Equally, It's OK to Be Great

We're fairly rubbish at sharing thoughts, feelings and emotions, aren't we? We have a tendency to hide feelings and this habit we have got into has not had a positive effect on the mental wellbeing of many of us. I say 'us' because I have been totally guilty of this in the past. I even still am sometimes.

I think it's natural for us not to want to burden people or share things because we feel silly or ashamed, but do you know what, as the saying goes, 'It's OK not to be OK.' Whilst I do often still play my emotional cards close to my chest, I have learned that sharing with those close to me and being honest with myself that I'm not OK is perfectly fine; in fact, it's good.

Being honest about how you feel lets people relate to you and, most importantly, allows the right people into your life to support you. We all need to find our right 'tribe'. Often those from the most unlikely sources become some of the greatest people in your life.

Whilst we're quick to hide our troubles and sadness from the world, strangely we also seem to shy away from sharing all the great things in our life, too. Whilst it really is OK not to be OK, it's equally OK to feel great and celebrate success. Be honest about your success and brilliance because it makes you feel good and proud. Anyone that can't get on board and support you in your success can, to be quite frank, do one.

We should celebrate all the little wins in life and take time to appreciate them because this can give us motivation and incentive to go even further – and you need to be your own number one fan and champion. If others don't like it, that's their problem and they're probably only jealous. Remember what we said about other people's opinions: not your concern.

What little win have you got to celebrate? Make a list and celebrate them all. It doesn't have to be with a huge party: a cuppa and five minutes' peace and quiet is just as deserved a celebration.

vi. Comparison Syndrome

Much of our failure to share good and bad things comes from an overriding issue called comparison syndrome. We all suffer from it at one point or another, so don't think that you're the only one feeling this way.

In this day and age, we are surrounded with images of the so-called 'perfect' everything in magazines, social media and on TV. Whether it's the perfect family, perfect figure, perfect home or perfect job, this ideal of perfection is everywhere – and what happens? We start to compare our life, careers, bodies and lifestyle to the edited showreel that belongs to others.

Let's get this very clear: there is no perfect. We should not aim for perfection either because it does not exist. What we should be aiming for is improvement and being incredibly proud of everything we achieve and who we all are as individuals; then sharing this brilliance with the world. If it's your own health, fitness, figure, family, home or life you're comparing, then understand no one is you. You are unique and incomparable, so just find confidence to do what is right for you, not for anyone else. More on 'perfection' later.

If it's your career or business, don't compare yourself or think you're not as good as someone else doing the same as you. Whilst healthy competition is good, there is room for everyone to be brilliant; you just have to find your niche, target market and happy place to thrive.

Try and get out of the mindset of comparing and move into the mindset of creativity.

vii. Stress

A two-minute walk from our houseboat in Italy, there is a bar at the side of the lake called *Pescatore*. This is one of my favourite places to go to work, relax and people watch, whilst soaking up the sun with a gentle breeze off the lake and an Aperol Spritz (rude not to!). The thing I love most about *Pescatore* is the way that the bar totally lives up to and feels likes its motto. *No stress* is the tag line of this bar and, honestly, as soon as you get there, you feel the stress washing away.

Stress is one of the worst things in life we have to endure. For some people, it can be crippling and debilitating, whilst others may only feel mild worry; either way, we've all experienced stress. Stress is a natural feeling, but it's the way we respond to it that causes us the most damage. Like with all negative emotions we experience, we try to fight the feeling of stress, as opposed to accepting and embracing it. What's even worse is the amount of stress WE add onto ourselves.

Why do we do this to ourselves when we know how much pain and anguish stress can cause us? Be it deadlines, comparison syndrome, time management, financial or work-related targets or health- and fitness-related goals, we are guilty of piling extra stress on ourselves at every juncture.

The more we try to be like others (heading down that comparison syndrome avenue again) the more stress we will put on ourselves – unnecessarily, too. Then follows the snowball effect that stress has on our mental and physical wellbeing and our personal and professional relationships. Most of all, it can make us hate ourselves and fail to function as best we can.

But how can we combat stress? There's no magic cure, but reducing stress starts with YOU. Think about these points when it comes to lowering your stress levels:

- Be kind to yourself and give yourself a break.
- Don't compare yourself to others. You are unique.
- Put yourself and your mental and physical wellbeing first.
- Take time each day for YOU ahead of anyone else's demands.
- Do what you love and love what you do.

When we take control of our own minds and bodies in a bid to start controlling our stress levels, our minds will become free and see the endless possibilities that can help us exist in our own world of less stress and anxiety. It will open us up to opportunities such as delegating tasks and hiring people to ease the workload, thus making us more productive, creating better schedules, managing our time in a way that benefits us and, importantly, prioritising our own health and wellbeing to give us a more balanced outlook.

Control your own mind and stress levels. Don't let them control you.

viii. Relax

Relax, chill out, take it easy. Sound familiar? These phrases or pearls of wisdom have probably been dished out to you in the same volume they have to me; and whilst you are appreciative of the concern and sentiment, saying those things does not help when you are feeling like a coiled spring and ready to burst. Correct? I mean, why didn't I just think of *chilling out* when the pressure was on? Well, if I had the time, I would have done but it's not just like turning a dial to the 'off' or 'relax' position.

So how can we relax whilst we're dealing with the tumultuous pile of stress in our lives? The fact is you can't, so we need to pre-empt it by putting ourselves first. Now, I know that the concept of self-care is still considered inherently selfish in British culture, but if we don't look after ourselves first, how can we deal with not only everything thrown at us but also the needs of others?

Later in the book, under Productivity, I will talk about balance and doing the things for you first every day to get in the right mindset. Each day you do the things for *yourself* first, you don't just talk about it – whether it's a simple cuppa in a quiet room, five minutes of TV, yoga, meditation, a run, anything that is purely for you. It's not selfish: it's necessity.

Factor this time into your schedule at the start of every day and build on it. Exercise, health and wellbeing are the most important things for your relaxation, but having time to yourself to strengthen your mind and body and set you up for the day ahead is invaluable. This strength will in turn not only make you feel balanced but much more relaxed.

The Three Ps

Possibility

Productivity

Performance

When I was at a weak point with my mental health (and not for the first time) I knew I had to find a sustainable way to get mentally fit again. By giving my mind space, time and support, I created a strategy that worked not just for my mental fitness but for my professional, business and private life.

The key word here is *sustainable.* Like anything, whether it's losing weight, exercise or anything of a habitual nature, you have to find something that is sustainable and which you can maintain. Like diets, quick fixes and fads don't work when you're trying to get your mental health in better shape. My strategy continues to work for me – and others – because it is wholly maintainable in hectic lives and all it takes is an adaption to your mindset.

The strategy is The Three Ps: Possibility, Productivity & Performance. Yes, that's it, it starts with you believing you can make something happen, creating a plan to make it happen and then actually making it happen.

7

Possibility

Ever had someone say to you that anything is possible but thought not for me, it's not?

I think we've all been in that position where we think only other people have amazing things happen to them or that we're not as lucky as the next person (that's the comparison syndrome kicking in again!), but actually, within reason, most things are possible.

The dictionary definition of possibility is 'a thing that may happen or be the case'.

Are you now thinking *may happen* ... then again it *may not* happen? Have you just reverted back to that thought that amazing things only happen to other people and not you? So, what's the difference between those people who something *may* happen to and those it *may not*? Well, it's nothing to do with luck or finances or any other excuse people want to throw around, but it has everything to do with mindset.

In order for something to be possible for you to achieve, first of all you have to be inspired to accomplish it. Once you have been inspired, this is where you then take control of your own thoughts and emotions and choose to have a great mindset. With a good mindset in place, it's time to set some amazing goals and then go nail them.

Just remember one thing: if you permanently live within your comfort zone, nothing will change for you, but with small steps and continually and consistently being productive, you will experience the changes and success you set your heart on.

i. Inspiration

In my opinion, being inspired is one of the greatest things we can experience. It can set us off on our own path of adventure. Inspiring others is one of the greatest free gifts we can give as humans. Inspiration can come to us in many ways, be it reading, writing, listening, thinking, eating, travelling, walking or meditating. You can be inspired by people and places, tastes and sounds. You can allow all your senses to be inspired.

I have been fortunate to be inspired by so many things throughout my life. When I was young, I was inspired by my father. I have been inspired by music, countries I've visited, food I've eaten, books I've read and the words of my late husband, Simon. Each wonderful moment of inspiration has led me to find something within myself to achieve my own success; my inspiration is what helps me be productive and ultimately perform. But what inspires me will not necessarily be the same as what inspires you. You need to find your own inspiration.

But often there is confusion between inspiration, motivation and influence. Quite simply, inspiration is something you feel from within, motivation is an external element or factor that gets you going and influence is what makes you go in a particular direction.

To share some examples, I was inspired by the emotions I felt towards the work of the amazing doctors and nurses that treated my husband for cancer and by other patients and families that I saw with their own cancer stories; I was motivated to fundraise for the Yorkshire Cancer Centre to do something to help and give something back; I was influenced by friends to sign up for the London Marathon. Hence, in 2019, I am running the Virgin

London Marathon in aid of the Yorkshire Cancer Centre, Bexley Wing at St. James's University Hospital, Leeds.

Essentially, you can be inspired to have an idea, but unless you put the work in, that idea will not blossom into anything.

In the words of the great American President John F. Kennedy: *Every accomplishment starts with the decision to try.*

ii. Goals

I read a great book a while ago called *The Art of Being Brilliant*, written by two guys named Andy Cope and Andy Whittaker. It was one of those easy reads that's resonated with me as everything made sense. There was nothing I didn't know, but it was delivered in a way that made me look at things with a slightly different perspective, and now it's one of my go-to book recommendations for anyone looking for a little clarity in their life or business.

One thing referenced in the book is 'HUGGS'. As Andy Cope said, 'Everyone needs a HUGG.' Yes, they do, Andy. Yes, they do! Now, yes, I am a hugger. I love a good cuddle, but I'm careful to gauge whether other people are huggers or handshakers! However, this HUGG is not the wrap your arms as tightly as you can around someone type hug, but a Huge Unbelievable Great Goal. So, yes, everyone needs a HUGG. What's your HUGG?

Goal setting often comes as a consequence of being inspired, but your personal and professional goals can also push and inspire you. Whether it's saving for the holiday of a lifetime, going self-employed, breaking a life-changing habit or planning to be debt-free, your massive goal should really push the boundaries of success and achievement and engage the services of creativity, passion and strategy and, of course, The Three Ps: Possibility, Productivity & Performance.

I don't just advocate having one huge goal but also some short, mid and long-term goals. There are so many ways to break these down: following a 90-day goal plan can be a good way to get started as 90 days is a great length of time to invest in a new project or concept. It's not too daunting an amount of time nor is it too short that you won't see results.

Of course, the most important thing when setting your goals is to ask yourself the following question: What do YOU want? Don't set your goals based on what you think others want you to do or think you should achieve. Put yourself first and ask exactly what you want to achieve for YOU, because I guarantee that if you put yourself and your needs first, you will be stronger for those around you. It is absolutely not selfish to put yourself first.

I think goals should never be easy, they should force you to work, even if they are uncomfortable at the time. Michael Phelps, Olympic swimmer.

Got your goals in mind? Good. Make a list and now let's get you geared up to achieve them.

iii. Mindset

Never forget, it is your choice as to whether you do things with a good attitude. We can't control or dictate situations, but we can control how we deal with them. You and you alone are responsible for ensuring your own mind and body are strong enough to deal with any situation thrown at you.

I have had so many days when I have woken up after a bad night's sleep and wanted to do nothing other than hide away from the world, hoping that if I ignore bad situations, they will go away. Guess what? They never do; and ignoring things only makes matters worse in the long run.

Once you have your inspiration and goals in place, the only thing standing between you achieving the success you crave is your frame of mind and the practical strategy you have in place. First things first, mindset is everything.

I get it, you're thinking:

It's not as easy as just being positive and things will happen.
My situation is harder than yours, you don't understand.
You're just a happy and positive person, it's easy for you.
There's no point in trying to achieve my goals or what I want. I'm unlucky and nothing ever goes right for me.

Any of those sound familiar? They do to me. I've probably thought or said them all at some point in my life and I've definitely heard other people say them, but I've come to realise that, actually, all of those statements are borne out of either laziness or fear.

I've learned the hard way that mindset is everything because, do you know what, contrary to what people think of me, it's been flipping hard. I've dealt with death too many times at different stages of my life, failure, divorce, mental health issues, more failure, low self-esteem, complete self-hatred, bullying and more, so the pity party doesn't wash with me. The only thing that gets me through every day is my positive mindset. I am choosing to succeed at my goals, not necessarily always on first attempt, but the failures and the lessons they've taught me along the way ultimately make me stronger and help in my eventual arrival at my destination. I choose to *win or learn*. To me, positivity doesn't mean things will turn out OK, rather that I will be OK regardless of how things turn out. The same can be said for you if you adopt a positive mindset.

Sometimes it's hard to engage a positive mindset. Many books have been written on the subject which go into it in far better and more qualified detail than I ever could. *The Chimp Paradox* by Professor Steve Peters helps you get your inner 'chimp' under control. You've probably met your chimp quite a few times: he's the pesky little thing that makes you do stupid things without thinking or makes you *react* rather than *respond* to situations – and not always in the best way. The book is a great training guide for mindset.

Maybe you struggle to adopt a positive mindset because of what's gone on in the past? I can admit to that. At my lowest, broken by people I'd once considered friends, it took me years to have the belief that I could control my mindset and actually achieve MY goals, because I'd been battered down to believe I was worthless, insignificant and useless. 'Judgey' people are the worst. I know we all can be a little judgemental – hands up to that one – but people who are judgemental to the point of destroying others do not deserve the time and space of anyone's mind. They definitely don't get space in mine anymore – though I do admit to a few wobbles now and again.

The thing that finally made my mindset flip from being weak due to the actions of other people to being confident, strong and positive was quite a simple realisation although it did take several years for it to be solidified in my mind. The acknowledgement was that several years on (years that I spent beating myself up and being scared by the words and opinions of others) I had actually changed myself and my life. Even when I was feeling weak in mind, every day I was growing and learning and developing: I was *winning and learning*. I was becoming stronger and achieving success, even if it didn't always feel like it. I was failing and learning from my mistakes. The biggest most mind-blowing discovery for me was the fact that not a single one of those judgemental and mean people had moved on with their lives at all.

I know I've already mentioned this lots, but it's important. Over the years, whilst I had met new people, learned so much, listened, talked, developed, failed and succeeded, they had gone nowhere and, as I look at them today, they are the same people, doing the same things, in the same place. Essentially, they are unhappy in their own lives and to make themselves feel better, they attack anyone who is willing to step out of their comfort zones. They are living in a small box where they have chosen not to grow. I want to live outside of a box; there's plenty of time to be in a box when I'm dead.

I'm not saying they are wrong to live their whole lives in one place – with the same people, with the same cyclic lifestyle, week in, week out – they just don't get to judge my life and they definitely don't get to criticise, comment and bring me down just as I don't get to criticise them. I acknowledge and respect their decisions may be good for them. Let's just co-exist and go about our own business.

This was the mindset game changer for me. It gave me the strength to focus on myself first as opposed to worrying about what they'd think; it gave me the strength to control my own mindset; and I'm choosing to have a great positive attitude, to live my life and to achieve my goals.

I doubt, even if they read this book, any of these people would click I could be referring to them; if they did, I would take that as a positive self-awareness for them and maybe they'd think twice about how they treat other people who aren't in their clique! (Cue paranoid messages on publication of book!).

If you're struggling with moving on in life and letting go of things that have happened, then a really good book to read is *S.U.M.O. (Shut Up, Move On)* by Paul McGee. It's subtitled *The Straight-Talking Guide to Succeeding in Life* and it's straight to the point. Maybe I should take this as a cue. Next chapter?

I'll tell you a little about the concept of *S.U.M.O.* first, though. *S.U.M.O.* is based on real life and encourages you to deal with your life as it is, not as you think it should be, and so reflection, recovery, responsibility, resilience, relationships, resourcefulness and reality become the seven factors which are all critical in us achieving better results in our lives.

McGee also reminds us that any outcome of a situation is based purely on our emotion and response. You may hear me mention a few times about acting on situations as opposed to reacting to them. McGee defines this with his equation E+R=O (Emotion + Response = Outcome). Taking time not to act instantly when something happens, but to take a breath and give a considered action will stand you and your mindset in much better stead.

Other areas McGee touches on for keeping your mindset in good check are not playing the victim role, Hippo Time (allowing yourself time to wallow when something happens but then moving on with your life) and the fact that understanding does not mean agreeing: you can see someone else's point of view without having to embrace that viewpoint yourself. That's a great consideration when keeping your mindset in check. Being a people pleaser and going along with things, even if you don't agree, can send your head and life into a spin and have a negative effect on your mental wellbeing, so know that it's perfectly OK for everyone to have their own views and beliefs. All you have to do is understand them, not agree with them.

I could write and talk about this for quite a while yet, but if you're looking for some mindset inspiration with regards to how you approach life and work, then look no further than *Fish* by Stephen C. Lundin, Harry Paul and John Christensen. In fact, go one better and look up *Fish Philosophy* on YouTube and check out the attitude of the people working at the Pike Place Fish Market in Seattle. This *Fish* philosophy is now global, being applied to lives, businesses and schools around the world. It's incredible and it's all based on four practices designed by the fishmongers, who choose to enjoy their work and make it fun, regardless of the rather cold and miserable early morning conditions.

The four practices are:

1. Choose Your Attitude

2. Play

3. Make Their Day

4. Be There

Apply these four principles to your life, even without doing any further research into them, and you've got an instant mindset flip. I really recommend you check them out.

The *Fish* philosophy embraces the idea that you choose how to work, live and act and you get to have fun with it. You can add value to other people's lives by making a difference, you can be there for yourself and others and you can choose to love what you do. That's mindset: making the choices about what and how you do things for the benefit of yourself. By engaging a good mindset and putting yourself first, you not only help others but you open yourself up to a vast array of possibilities.

We are shaped by our thoughts; we become what we think. When the mind is pure, joy follows like a shadow that never leaves. Buddha.

iv. The Art of Possibility

When it comes to the subject of possibility, the teachings of the great orchestral conductor Benjamin Zander and the book he wrote with his wife, Rosamund, *The Art of Possibility,* have taught me more about possibility than any other single resource. I use the book as a reference for the learning of myself and others on a weekly basis. Isn't it wonderful to have a go-to resource that never fails to inspire? That's why I wanted to share a little about the book here and felt it deserved its own chapter.

The book is full of energy, stories, anecdotes and both personal and powerful breakthrough practices for creativity; and creativity is one of our biggest superpowers in The Three Ps. The Zanders' *The Art of Possibility* embraces a series of lessons, commencing with the principle that 'it is all invented'. What is invented you may ask? Well, essentially everything. Once you get your head round that idea, you can enter a whole world of possibilities.

Invention in this context means that:

- There is no correct or perfect method to getting things done.
- Everything is invented and you can invent your own way of achieving your best outcome.
- You can reach the same outcome many ways. After all, both 2+2 and 1+3 = 4.

There is an old creative thinking puzzle which Zander references. It may be one you know already. Its value is in making you realise that by thinking creatively, you can actually achieve things that seem impossible.

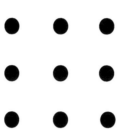

Instructions

Using four straight lines, join up all the dots without your pen leaving the paper. Simple!

Hint

Don't be afraid to think creatively and out of the box, quite literally!

I'm just going to leave this with you! If you want to know more about it, then check out the Zanders' book – or stop and ask me one day!

The next part of *The Art of Possibility*, which I use in a lot of my coaching and mentoring, is Benjamin Zander's concept of giving yourself an A. I personally think this should be something implemented not only into our own lives but into every education system around the world. We need to be kind to ourselves in order to achieve success in our life or work. When we are kind and honest with ourselves, we open ourselves up to possibility and from here, with a productive strategy and hard work, we can achieve anything with our greatest performances.

Giving yourself an A was inspired by Benjamin Zander who, at the start of the new academic year at the university he taught at, told his students they had all gained an A grade before they started the course; all they had to do was keep it. Instantly, the students were working from a place of possibility and success rather than struggling to work up to getting an A. This allowed them to achieve great success and exceed their own expectations. All he requested of them was to write a letter to him, dated 12 months later, detailing exactly how they achieved this amazing grade. This became their accountability and inspiration and 12 months after writing the letter, success was achieved. Why? Because they had the success within them from the start and maintaining the grade and flourishing was all that was left to do.

So often we compare ourselves to others who are doing the same or similar things as us and this, along with our fear of failure, can lead us to think we are not worthy of being the best. We try to compete, but really the only competition we should have is within ourselves, to be a better version of ourselves each day.

By using Zander's method of giving ourselves an A, we live our life from a perspective of achievement. We act as if we have already achieved our goal and this in turn gives us more confidence and further encouragement to achieve even more success and happiness; and we are much kinder to ourselves due to our outlook of possibility and success.

There are so many other aspects of *The Art of Possibility* that I could write about, but I really recommend you read it for yourself! It places a huge importance on contribution, which is a pivotal point when we are trying to achieve success, balance and happiness. Often, we put so much pressure on ourselves to achieve things single-handedly that we burn ourselves out quickly, leading to an imbalance both mentally and physically, whereas if we focussed on being a contribution we could achieve much more. Ask for the help, share a problem, run an idea past a friend, hire a personal assistant, ask someone to watch the children for an hour so you can go for a run. Whatever it is, let yourself and others be a contribution to a bigger picture and you will soon start to see this not only makes more things possible for you and everyone around you, but you will feel much more centred, balanced and, yes, you guessed it: happy!

The Art of Possibility makes you realise that anything is possible, but you have to take action to make it possible, and as with The Three Ps, possibility is followed by productivity, which will lead you to a fabulous performance.

No matter what, people grow. If you choose not to grow, you're staying in a small box with a small mindset. People who win go outside of that box. It's very simple when you look at it. Kevin Hart, actor.

8

Productivity

In my experience, when someone asks how you're doing, one of the most common answers after 'I'm fine' is 'I'm busy'. I'll hold my hands up to having given this response (well, both of them actually!) as it's easy and doesn't require any further communication, but the response 'I'm busy' frustrates me, even when I say it myself!

You see, being busy is not necessarily a positive thing. I want people to be happy and successful and achieve everything they want to, but I don't want them to be 'busy'. Quite simply, I want all of you to be productive and not busy.

There's no difference, I hear you say. Oh, but there is, a massive life-changing difference, courtesy of the two words productive and busy.

Being busy will eventually cloud your mind and judgement and burn you out. Being busy doesn't allow for time and space in your own head and consequently affects your mental and physical wellbeing. Being busy will not help you achieve everything you want to achieve, be that success or happiness. However, productivity will.

Being productive means you have seen what's possible and you're taking some action towards achieving your goal. Being productive means you are working smarter, not harder. Being productive allows you to find balance, success and happiness in your life as you have time and space not only in your own head but also in your personal and professional life so you can do and achieve more.

If you look the words up in a dictionary, you may find definitions similar to these:

busy – having a great deal to do

productive – achieving a significant amount or result

Now do you see the life-changing difference between *busy* and being *productive*. Which would you rather be? For me, it's definitely productive because I want time and flexibility to live my life on my terms, in my way, and do all the exciting things on my bucket list, and spend time with my friends whilst running my business and making a success of my professional career, as opposed to being worn down by the grind of just being busy and not doing all the things I want to for me.

The only real way to achieve the success you want, whether that is work-related, going on a luxury holiday or mastering a yoga move, is to action your plans and ideas. This is going to take a few different elements coming together, such as balance, discipline and strategy.

I'm going to go into some detail in specific areas which will help action your plans and ideas.

i. Balance

Balance is absolutely key to everything. Imagine a set of the old-fashioned kitchen scales. Put too much on one side and it drops downwards fast; too much on the other side and everything shifts too far in the other direction. In order to keep everything functioning, we need to find that equilibrium. This theory needs to be applied to life as well.

Some areas where balance needs to be applied are between work and play, 'me' and 'we' time, serious and fun, and goodness and treats. For so long my balance was totally out of kilter. I'd focus on all the wrong things, working to constant deadlines, pleasing others, too much seriousness and carrying everyone else's stress. The consequence was I lost myself, was unhealthy, unproductive, miserable and anxious: not a good mix. I'd jump out of bed, straight to the computer in the early hours doing important jobs but could then be there for hours, without breaks and feeling fairly unfulfilled by it all. By the time I realised, a whole day had gone past and despite having ticked off lots from my to-do list, I felt like I'd achieved nothing for me.

I'm an avid reader and had read numerous books referencing the 'power hour' and getting things done first in the morning. Whilst I'm a fan of the *Eat that Frog* mentality (read it, it's a great book by Brian Tracy that gets you to stop procrastinating and get the big things done first each day) and I'm quite good at getting up and doing things first thing in the morning, the older and more experienced in life I was getting the more I was feeling that this approach was less maintainable for me and not keeping me in the best mindset all day (see the later chapter on Mornings).

63

I realised that in order to be truly productive I needed balance and that meant tipping the scales to put me first, getting my mindset in the best place by doing what I want to do first and then cracking on with things that had to be done. In his book *How to be F*cking Awesome,* writer and mentor Dan Meredith talks about doing YOUR things first each day to get into a good mindset to deal with everything in your day-to-day life and then to work in two shorter blocks of time in the morning and afternoon to be more productive – and it works! I've been utilising this method myself for quite some years now.

Balance YOUR time, work, development time, exercise and wellbeing time, family time and, most importantly, nothing time. Time for doing absolutely nothing is really important. When was the last time you did that? Precisely nothing? Try it, it will make you feel really balanced and if you want more validation that it's OK to do your stuff first, read Dan's book. It's a belter.

ii. Discipline

Having discipline and boundaries is so important and that is both self-discipline and discipline with others. Without putting discipline and boundaries in place, our lives become a flustered mess with little vision for possibility and a lot less productivity. Sound familiar?

But discipline does not mean depravity. We don't want to deprive ourselves of anything at all, rather we want to install balance into our lives so we can experience true happiness. I don't know about you, but the thought of depriving myself of something to achieve success makes me less inclined to want to be successful! I'm anti my new regime before it's started. Plus, isn't it always the case that if you tell yourself you can't have something (be it cakes, alcohol or that new book you've been eyeing up), the first thing you actually crave is that thing!

If you're like me, you've probably tried numerous diets in a bid to get 'healthy' and lose weight. So many of these diets are based on depriving yourself of things; sometimes even depriving yourself of actual food! Does this make us happy? Well, a fleeting quick result that doesn't last may give us a moment of delight, but in reality, no, this doesn't make us happy. The process of deprivation makes us miserable and crave things all the more and the results are short-lived. But, if we took a disciplined approach to diet that allowed us to experience everything in moderation, we wouldn't feel deprived of anything during the diet process and the results would be a lot more successful and sustainable.

What does this tell us? Quite simply, that old adage of 'everything in moderation'.

Being disciplined is also about respecting yourself enough to put yourself first. Come on, hands up, who's a people pleaser? I'm definitely not judging you if you are because for most of my life, I've been guilty of trying to please everyone and putting other people's needs before my own, be it my family, friends, colleagues or strangers! Time and time again I would bend over backwards to help others before caring for myself and my own needs and where did it get me? In honesty, not very far at all and really it held me back for so long.

Putting other people's needs first has driven me to the edge of anxiety and depression. It has made me mentally, physically and financially unwell and unfit and had a huge negative effect on my whole life, my health and my relationships; yet, at the time, the need to be doing things for the benefit of other people before taking care of my own needs seemed more important to me. It was ridiculous really and there was a cycle that the more I did for others, the more normal and OK I thought that was, regardless of what I actually wanted or needed.

Then something changed for me. I got so low and struggled with so much, but with the support of my rather fabulous husband Simon, I slowly started putting boundaries in place and saying no to people. I put my own needs first and got disciplined with myself and others. My boundaries included simple changes such as 'office hours' so people couldn't expect responses at all hours, and I switched my laptop off at a designated time each day. This discipline was my saviour and it gave me time for me. People soon learned what I would and wouldn't respond to when, and what I would tolerate.

I also prioritised what I needed ahead of work. Each day I schedule my time in before work, whether that's exercise, reading, meditation, family time or 'nothing' time (it's really good to just do nothing sometimes!), then I'm very disciplined with my to-dos each day – between three and five each day (check out the chapter on Planning for more info on this) in two designated work slots. The result? I have more time for me and I work less but I am ultimately so much more productive, successful, healthier in mind and body and happier for it.

That is how and why discipline is vital! It can quite literally save you. My own experience has proved this to me, and you can make small changes for huge benefits as well. Let me share with you a few ideas to help you be more disciplined.

iii. Boundaries

Definition of *boundary* – a line which marks the limits of an area.

We all need our boundaries, and for me, as I previously mentioned, boundaries came in the form of set office hours stated on my email signatures, turning my laptop off at a set time each day, switching my phone to silent or off and being strict with the time frame in which I responded to messages and emails. (It is perfectly acceptable not to respond to work emails at midnight. Don't let people expect that immediate response from you 24/7: they neither expect or require it.) Put yourself before their demands. Likewise, don't send messages at ridiculous times of the day and put others in a position of needing to respond. Whilst you may think you're being organised, they may not have good boundaries in place. Respect other people's boundaries, as you wish yours to be respected.

I had lapsed into all the bad habits of being on-hand for everyone 24 hours a day, 7 days a week. Whilst it makes you seem super-efficient, it is in fact just making things worse for you personally as you're being constantly distracted, not getting the rest you need, not getting your 'me' time, not working to your strategies – all of which means you are not being productive.

It is an easy habit to slip in to, though, and when I recognised what I was doing to myself, I put some clear-cut boundaries in place, marking the limits of my area. The maintainable consequence of this was that my productivity rate shot up. I got far more done, slept more and I had more time for what I wanted to do. My business conversions were up, I had more time to spend with my close friends and family and I knew I was becoming productive as opposed to busy.

As a parent and having been a teacher, I know it's important to put boundaries in place with children so they know the limits of acceptability. I can assure you, it's equally important to set boundaries for adults, whether they be clients, colleagues, friends or family. People will respect the boundaries you have laid for the benefit of you, your life and your productivity and, to be quite simple, if they don't, then they don't deserve the benefits of your valuable time and attention.

iv. Distractions

Essentially, we want to move from distraction to action. When we are being productive, we don't need all those things around us that make our concentration wander and take our eye off our goal and the task in hand. If your goal, work or target requires you to sit down and work at a desk, then de-clutter; get rid of all the unnecessary gadgets, papers, stationery and books so the space around you is clear. Similarly, don't just get rid of the physical things, get rid of electronic and virtual ones, too.

If your work requires concentration and writing documents at a computer, switch off Wi-Fi so you can't distract yourself with two minutes on the internet; that two minutes is an hour of watching mindless cat videos before you know it!

Get rid of email and app notifications on your phone or computer. You know as soon as one comes in, you're going to check it, so don't tempt yourself and put your phone, iPad and computer on silent so you don't feel the urge to respond to messages and notifications (if you haven't already turned them off!) every two minutes. The time saved by making these small and easy changes is time in which you can be productive. It may feel tough at first, but be disciplined with yourself: it's worth it to make yourself more productive.

v. Sleep

We all need sleep – it's a basic human requirement – and whilst some people may be able to function on just a few hours, not all of us can. Those functioning on just a few hours' sleep every night because they are so 'busy' will soon feel those signs of burnout I mentioned before.

There has been so much research on sleep and sleep patterns and there is plenty of advice on the 'ideal' amount of sleep an adult or child requires, but some people really struggle with sleep due to physical issues or not being able to switch off at night. For some people, falling asleep in silence is paramount; whilst others like to have the TV on until they've drifted off. Some people like to read a book before bed; others will scan social media or play a game on their phone until lights out. Do what works for you. Regardless of your bedtime routine, though, the fact remains we want to get some good quality sleep in order to keep being as productive as possible.

I, possibly like many of you, wear a watch that monitors my daily activity and sleep patterns and I find it quite interesting to look at the results each day. As well as making sure I get to that ideal 10,000 steps target each day (now that's a daily battle!), this watch has helped give me an understanding of my sleep patterns. More often than not, I fall quickly into a deep sleep as soon as I turn my lights out. I usually manage around 10% of my total sleep time in a deep sleep, whilst the rest of my sleep pattern jumps about between the other stages of sleep.

My understanding of sleep patterns is this (please remember I am not an expert in this field): There are actually four stages of sleep that we usually pass through each night (or daytime if you've been working a night shift or battling jetlag!), known as stages 1, 2 and 3, followed by REM: rapid eye movement sleep. These stages work in cycles of between 90 to 120 minutes, moving from stage 1, the lightest stage, through to stage 2 and 3, the deepest stage, before heading backwards to stages 2 and 1 and then into REM, the dreaming stage. Got it? I think that's about right anyway, but do your own research if you're interested.

Now, here's the important part when it comes to your productivity. When your alarm goes off in the morning DO NOT press the snooze button! Why, you may ask? My very simplistic understanding and answer to this is because when you wake up that is a sleep cycle ended, so if you press snooze for 5 minutes you are lulling your body into the false idea it can go for another full cycle of sleep, so it's expecting 90–120 minutes, but you're only going to give it 5 minutes. If you then press snooze for a second, or even third, time, the same thing will happen and so on, until you eventually get out of bed. Consequently, your body becomes confused and you actually feel more tired than you should and you won't be nearly as productive as you'd like to be.

Please bear in mind, as I tell you once again, I'm not an expert. This is based on my experience and findings, but it makes logical sense to me and has explained why I feel better and more productive when either a) I wake up naturally without an alarm or b) I get out of bed as soon as my alarm goes off.

vi. Mornings

In the chapter about Balance, I talked about doing things for you first every day and how I'd realised that, for me, the idea of the 'power hour' or 'magic hour' first thing when I get up and go straight to work was not maintainable on a long-term basis.

Don't get me wrong, I've gone through long periods of time where I would purposefully get up an hour earlier than necessary to get a stack of work done at my computer and yes, it was great to crack on and shift the to-do list early doors, but I would feel myself flagging later in the day. On days when I also had to work in the evening, as a musician, until 10pm or later and then have a long drive home, I found the 5am start to the day draining. I just wasn't getting enough sleep and my productivity levels were dropping, even with an afternoon nap!

As a rule, I am an early riser, but that daily regime of going to my computer first thing to get that power hour of work in was pretty much killing me. I knew I had to change things to work better for me.

Yes, I know that there's research to say we are at our most creative in the morning and this is when we get our best work done in a day, but quite frankly, if you've not had enough sleep or aren't fully awake, you really aren't going to be all that creative or productive.

I did a little research into various things and read lots of different perspectives on the topic, too. I read some articles about sleep inertia, which made for interesting reading. Basically, sleep inertia is the groggy, rough feeling many people feel when they are waking up, which apparently can last for one minute to four hours, hence why some people bound out of bed and others take a little more time, several cuppas and a shower before they start to function. We are all unique. Research shows that the 'typical' amount of time is around 15–30 minutes.

So, what has this got to do with anything? Well, the thing about sleep inertia (which, by the way, is a normal part of life for most of us), regardless of how long it lasts, is that during this period your mind is running at a reduced capacity and therefore, even the simplest of tasks will not be done to your full potential. Having read about it, I started thinking about my own morning activities and whether I was actually fulfilling them to the max and if planning my day this way round was actually giving me my highest rate of productivity. The simple answer was no! Right then, time to change things up.

Us humans are not so keen on change, but I for one am all for it if it means making things better or more productive. In fact, I'm one of those people that believes failure is good because that is how we actually learn and develop. Remember what I mentioned in an earlier chapter that we don't fail, we either *win or learn.* Probably why I have learned so hard and fast!

There is a quote I often share, the words of US Navy officer and computer programmer Grace Hopper: *The most dangerous phrase in the English language is we've always done it this way.* I think this quote sums up the approach of many people along with *If it ain't broke, don't fix it.* Yet I want to change things regularly and for every day to be different because that's how we grow and don't get bored. Heavens, my business, Mode for... is built on the ethos developed by Simon and me of 'love what you do and do something you love and different every day'.

Change is good, change is necessary, change will get you where you really want to be. I knew I had, and wanted, to change my daily routine to maximise my productivity and that whilst that early morning power hour at my computer was getting things done, it wasn't serving me personally, so I put the early morning shift of my day to better use by dedicating it, and the next hour or so, to myself.

This didn't mean I got up later and have a great lie-in every day; no, I still rise early but I prioritise myself and my personal needs ahead of my lengthy to-do list. The new routine? Get up, cuppa, bit of morning TV, some exercise, shower, breakfast, read a bit of a book, have a scan through social media … right, a few hours have passed, I'm feeling creative and good to go. Let's get the computer on, get rid of the distractions and have a solid two hours working, with breaks to make a cuppa or cuddle a cat! Then it's lunchtime and a break and then another few hours' solid work in the afternoon and done for 4pm so I can have family time or a rest if I'm working that evening.

Granted, this full-day programme isn't possible every day due to my ever-changing routine and because every day is different. Whether I'm sat at my computer, out and about with clients, running a wedding or event or on holiday, my early mornings are now pretty standard.

The results of this change? Well, for me, the results were fantastic. Just taking time for me first thing in the morning put me in a positive mindset; I felt ready for everything on my to-do list and was ploughing ahead with a steamroller of productivity. Quite often I'll reserve the morning work slot for the big jobs (eating that frog), admin, emails and to-do list items (having planned my entire to-do list on a Sunday and allocated three to five items to each working day; another great tip advocated by mentor Dan Meredith) before spending the afternoon session on planning, development and writing.

I saw a shift in productivity by at least 50% if not more, all because I dared to throw away the rule books and put myself first at the start of the day. Not only was I more productive, my business was growing at a greater rate, I had more time for family and friends and I felt so much better and less tired. That tiny little change in the morning was a game changer.

Remember, you don't need to be like a light switch flicking straight on in the morning and shining bright straight away: it's perfectly OK to be a dimmer switch and warm up to that shine! Try it for yourself. Put yourself first and concentrate on your personal time first thing in the morning and see what a difference it makes to your productivity.

vii. Diet

Something else to be clear on straight from the off: I am not about to give any advice on food choices or suggest you need to go on a diet in order to be more productive. I am the last person to offer dietary advice and although I've spent time reading up on all things nutrition and own enough cookery books to open a shop, I am no expert in the field of diet and nutrition. However, I am going to say, again based on my own experiences and research, there is a correlation between food, nutrition and productivity and it's not just about what you eat either, but also when and how you eat.

I don't want to go into extensive detail, but the basic premise is by eating clean, eating regularly and drinking lots of fluid (no, this does not include alcohol sadly!) and not depriving yourself of treats, your body will function at its best in order to help you be as productive as possible. That's all we want: to function at our best.

You probably know yourself that when you're hungry it's harder to function and concentrate. Your brain gets easily distracted. It's just taken me five times longer than it should to write this chapter, purely because it's mid-afternoon and I'm in a between-meals-slump and every little thing is distracting me!

I believe that deprivation is not the answer to anything and balance is the key to it all. So, eat well and balanced, cover all the food bases, or macros as we now refer to them, and drink plenty of fluids and that will help keep you productive.

viii. Exercise

Continuing from the importance of a balanced and clean diet which allows everything in moderation (yes, I also believe a little red wine, gin and a few treats now and again are essential for my wellbeing and sanity!), exercise also plays an important role in keeping your productivity rates nice and high. Not just physical exercise though, exercise for both your mind and body.

As I write this book, I am training for the London Marathon in April 2019, when I will be running in memory of my husband for the Yorkshire Cancer Centre, the Bexley Wing at St. James's University Hospital, Leeds (side note – this place is absolutely incredible and we were so blessed and grateful to fall under its care for Simon's cancer).

At various points in my life I have been pretty fit, other times not so much, but when I'm dedicating a little time each week (at least 30 minutes, three times a week) I notice a huge leap in my productivity levels in comparison to days when the most exercise I do is get out of bed. In fact, though much of the time I would love nothing more than to be able to stay in watching TV or reading books on the sofa all day, when I should be exercising, I actually feel worse on days when I do nothing, and by the end of those days I really wished I'd made more effort to get the 10,000 steps in.

Exercise, though to many of us a tiresome chore, actually does make us feel better. The more you do, the more you want to do. Why? Because being active gives us more energy and boosts our concentration, drive, mental wellbeing, physical health and in turn also makes our productivity levels rocket. It's the endorphins! This is because when we move, our heart pumps faster, circulating more blood and oxygen to all our organs, including our brains. But it doesn't have to be vigorous weightlifting or running for miles (I hate running by the way, which makes this whole London Marathon experience quite bizarre indeed – but it's a challenge for a good cause), walking is one of the best forms of exercise we can get.

When I feel myself not just in need of physically moving, but also in need of getting thoughts moving in my head to spark more ideas or to get rid of a writing block, often I take myself for a walk. There is something about physically moving in the fresh air which really helps some mental movement. It feels like it gives my head space and time to think. I can look around and take everything in and I start to see details and colours again. The simple luxury of walking is not only beneficial to my physical health, but also my mental wellbeing and my productivity levels. I always find going for a walk is when I do some of my best thinking and planning; and what seemed like a big challenge in my head before I set off is soon a strategised plan and no issue at all.

Exercising our brains is just as important as our bodies, so anything that helps flex the strength of the grey matter is going to be great for your health, wellbeing, fitness and productivity. Reading, writing, playing music, drawing, dancing, acting, Sudoku, puzzles – anything that allows your mind to be stretched and creative is going to be a huge advantage to you in your mission to adopt The Three Ps into your lifestyle.

ix. Strategies

Strategies are your friend; well, if you want to be truly productive, they are anyway. A strategy is basically a plan of action designed to achieve a particular aim, but you already knew that. I don't want to state the obvious about what strategies are, but it genuinely astounds me how many people fail to have them in place, even when there's something they particularly want to achieve. Honestly, how can you achieve things without having a strategy in place to conquer your goals?

Is there a project you're working on or an issue in your life that's testing you and affecting your happiness? If so, you can work your way through any issues strategically. Implementing a plan is key to not only productivity and success but dealing with overwhelm and any problems you may have in life and work.

To implement a successful strategy, go through the following five steps:

- Struggle
- Search
- Solution
- System
- Success

Have you an issue you're trying to work through? Try implementing this process and work on each step individually to achieve your end goal. Know that what you want to achieve is possible, get productive and implement this plan and then go and perform each action. Once you've got your strategy in place, the next step is, quite simply, planning.

x. Planning

French writer and aviator Antoine de Saint-Exupéry was quoted as saying: *A goal without a plan is just a wish.*

To be productive and achieve our goals, we need to get a plan of action together, a plan that covers the following questions:

- What?
- Why?
- Where?
- When?
- How?

Being productive and focussed and carrying out your strategy takes planning, and the easiest way to do this is by having a good structure, organisation and regular procedures. Preparing a to-do list or checklist is a great way to keep on track and make your goals a reality, not just a wish, but we want to get you in the habit of a regular, maintainable system. What's important is to create a list that makes you productive but doesn't overwhelm you when you look at it.

That's why, as previously mentioned, I advocate planning your week to have between three and no more than five things on your to-do list each day. Most importantly, add a 'why' you want to do these things. Adding a reason or a why means the task really matters to you and you can see the benefit of doing it. It will drive you towards your overall goal more efficiently. I call this my 'five a day' and we know five a day is good for you!

Here's an exercise to help you with your planning:

Instructions

Fill in the following box with all the ideas in your head which are things that need doing or will enhance your life or business.

Hint

This is your inspiration list. A great time to write it down is on a Sunday. It gets everything out of your head and onto paper. I actually start filling it as and when things pop into my head the week before.

Next

Grade the things in the above box in order of importance. You can colour code, use numbers 1–3 or letters a–c, whatever works for you. Then go through the items, putting between three and five in the box below, from Monday to Friday. Start with the most important things first, spreading them out over the week, then add in the not-so important things. Now, each day you have a productive plan of action. Cross things off as you complete them and feel the satisfaction and sense of achievement.

Remember

Don't try and make the tasks too big. You want to be pushed to be productive but you want to actually achieve the tasks each day – and you certainly don't want to be overwhelmed. They can be a mix of work, family and things for YOU!

Monday	Task	Why?
	1.	
	2.	
	3.	
	4.	
	5.	
Tuesday	1.	
	2.	
	3.	
	4.	
	5.	
Wednesday	1.	
	2.	
	3.	
	4.	
	5.	
Thursday	1.	
	2.	
	3.	
	4.	
	5.	
Friday	1.	
	2.	
	3.	
	4.	
	5.	

The Point?

The point is to build a structured system that you can rely on and use each week to make every day productive. The sense of achievement in completing all tasks each day is a great motivator and will inspire you to progress to the next day and through your week with enthusiasm. It's your life and work five a day!

Another great planning tool you could try is a well-known system called the **Eisenhower Box**. The Eisenhower Box is a to-do list system, which allows you to refine your to-do list by dividing it up into four categories:

Important & Urgent	Important & Not Urgent
Not Important & Urgent	Not Important & Not Urgent

The system works like this:

- **Important & Urgent** – Things to DO NOW
- **Important & Not Urgent** – Things to PLAN
- **Not Important & Urgent** – Things to DELEGATE
- **Not Important & Not Urgent** – Things to DELETE

By implementing and planning systems like these, you will increase your productivity, efficiency and available time, and decrease your stress. That has to be a winning combination.

xi. Delegation

When planning and discussing our business Mode for... my husband Simon would always say that the only way to grow and develop the business was to get other people to do things. I totally agree with this and it's also my belief that as a small, or large, business owner, you have to work 'on' your business and not 'in' it in order to develop. It can be hard letting go, handing over the reins and putting trust in someone else, and I'm not just talking about assigning tasks if you run your own business. The same applies to our personal lives.

Historically and naturally, I am one of those people who would do everything by themselves and take on the strain rather than burdening someone by asking for help. Whilst I still have this tendency, Simon was the first person who taught me it was OK to ask for help, to delegate tasks and that I didn't need to do everything myself.

I know I'm not the only one that's like this. Whether it's a child in school who would rather struggle than put their hand up in class to ask a question, a new mum who thinks they are a failure if they ask for a few hours' break from their baby to catch up on cleaning or have an afternoon nap or a business owner who thinks they have to do everything alone because they can't afford to hire someone else, there are millions of us whose go-to move is to struggle on by ourselves.

To all of you wonderful people that I may have just described, I say this to you:

Ask the question in class, it's the only way you will learn and develop.

Ask a friend or family member to babysit for a few hours; you need rest and your space to function at your best for you and your family.

Don't be scared to hire in help; your time is worth money and by paying someone else you could be saving yourself money and growing at the same time.

Don't be scared of losing control. Delegating is not about losing control but in fact empowering people and surrounding yourself with people you can trust.

Surround yourself with the best people you can find, delegate authority, and don't interfere as long as the policy you've decided upon is being carried out.

These words of former US President Ronald Reagan bring home the point that if you delegate, you have to give people your trust to carry out the delegated tasks.

Entrusting the smallest of tasks can make a huge difference to your life, giving you more time to develop your business, and boosting your productivity levels no end. Whether it's allocating household chores, hiring a virtual assistant for a few hours a week, engaging the services of a cleaner or gardener or asking someone to do some of the driving so you don't have to, even getting your shopping delivered, every little task that you can delegate is going to ease the personal pressure on yourself and that's what we want to do in order to help you be more productive.

Take a look at your day-to-day life. What tasks could you pass on? Don't overanalyse the situation, just start delegating and see what a difference it makes. If you're not sure what tasks to hand over, refer back to the Eisenhower Box in the chapter on Planning. Anything on your weekly task list which is not important and urgent is your list of tasks to delegate.

Remember: anything which is not important and not urgent quite simply needs deleting off your list. It's not going to service your life or needs and definitely not your productivity if it's not important and not urgent.

xii. STOP – Assess and Check In

STOP…

How often in a day do you actually stop and check in with yourself?

What do you mean check in with yourself? I hear you asking! Well, I mean how often do you stop each day and ask yourself what's good, what's bad, what could be tweaked to make the day better?

We all have busy lives and sometimes it's easy to fly through a day and not once take time for ourselves, let alone ask ourselves how we are doing. If we met up or chatted with a friend, one of the first things we'd probably do is ask how they are. Yet somehow, we often fail to extend this courtesy to ourselves and, quite frankly, if you don't take care of yourself first and be kind to yourself, how can you expect anyone else to?

The importance of checking in with yourself is not just a great habit to get into for your own mental and physical wellbeing but also for your productivity. Taking just two minutes a few times a day to stop and ask yourself how things are going or how your day could be developed could be a real game changer for your productivity levels. That two minutes could allow you to see what's great, what could be better and to re-direct your day and actions into a more positive path.

For example, you may have planned to have a good few hours dedicated to one task in the morning, but you left the TV on and got distracted by daytime TV so didn't get as much done as you wanted. If you were to take just two minutes to stop and notice this, you could address the issue and, in the afternoon, switch off the TV so that distraction is not an issue.

When stopping and checking in with yourself, you may realise you're not happy with a situation or that a task you're doing is actually neither important nor urgent. Now you have the opportunity to address that situation. If you hadn't have stopped, you would have carried on out of habit for the full day, wasting your time and energy and not being productive.

Taking a moment to stop is, as I just touched on, also good for your mental and physical wellbeing. When you stop, close your eyes and take a few deep breaths in through your nose and out through your mouth. This will ground you and will realign your mind and body, lowering any anxiety levels and bringing clarity for you to then check in with yourself. If you've been sat working at your desk or been deeply involved with a particular task, also use this opportunity of stopping to get up and stretch or move a few paces. I know how easy it is to get so engrossed that before you know it, hours have passed and you haven't moved or even had a glass of water. Be disciplined with yourself, check in often and help yourself to elevate your productivity levels and your mental and physical health.

With your goals and tasks created and your habits and strategies for productivity securely in place, there's only one thing left to do now: get performing.

9

Performance

Perfection is not attainable, but if we chase perfection, we can catch excellence. Vince Lombardi, American football player and coach.

When it comes to it, you have to realise that perfection is a myth. We should actually aim for improvement, not perfection, in ourselves, work and life in order to find our true happiness. The moment you realise and accept this is the moment you release a huge pressure off yourself. You will start to enjoy, smile, develop, actually find happiness and perform.

I am a professionally trained musician and a joy of performing is within me, but when I refer to 'performance' I do not just mean getting up on stage and playing to thousands of people. I mean the performance that is our everyday life and business, getting up each day and executing the tasks we have defined through our possibility and productivity.

Our performance is what is going to make us achieve our goals, however big or small they are, regardless of whether it is as a musician, a mum, a student, someone embracing grief, someone dealing with anxiety and depression or a business owner (I have been or am all of these!). For me, there are four main components we need to focus on to help create our best performance:

- Confidence – believe in yourself
- Competence – be an authority in your field
- Clarity – get your message across
- Communication – make yourself understandable

It's the Four Cs to go with our Three Ps!

As a child, I was taught music by my father and then went on to study music at school and at some of the best music conservatoires in the UK. I worked hard and was pushed for perfection, rarely achieving such a thing. When you didn't give a flawless musical performance, it was sometimes deemed to be failure. I often performed competitively and the mere hint of a grazed note in a performance would lead to the blatant and loud gasps of the audience. The reactions you come to expect are more terrifying than the performance itself (which can be said of life, when we worry more about what people will think than the actual job in hand). Yet still you strive for that perfection. Certainly, in a competitive musical world, the desire for perfection can begin to cloud the actual joy of making music.

Then, quite some years ago, it occurred to me that this perfection we are striving for doesn't exist. A live music performance should show humility, emotion, passion and belief and none of these things are perfect; they are honest, emotional and 'real' elements that make up a performance. I would much rather listen to a musician who connected with me as the audience and showed true emotions as opposed to a musician who gave a contrived but seemingly perfect performance with no communication. After all, what is music if it is without emotion? Music is what feelings sound like.

The same is true for any walk of life, not just music. Honesty and passion will connect with people much more than perfection. A person will make friends quicker – and with the right people – if they are honest about who they are, rather than trying to be someone they think they should be. A business owner will strike up a better deal with a more compatible colleague or client if they are honest and avoid trying to be bigger and better than they actually are. You will learn to live with grief or anxiety more easily if you talk about it and embrace it as opposed to trying to hide it and pretending to be 'perfectly fine'.

Striving for perfection can make us fake. It makes us less honest and may lead us to 'perform' as something we are not. Our performances in life, business and all that we do need to be truthful and honest and, above all, personal. Never forget that your story is unique. Your story will inspire others, so don't be afraid to tell your story. Whatever you are striving for, give your most honest performance.

Don't float through life on autopilot, doing what you think is right or expected or trying to fit in. Be conscious and in the moment. Be aware of what's around you and the people with whom you are interacting, and love what you do, whether that's to a crowd of thousands or at home to an audience of your cat!

Having your strategy in place is a great thing, but the plan is only going to be brilliant and successful if it's communicated well to your audience. As every musician will tell you, a good performance is created by constructive rehearsal; and since the strategy you have just created is your rehearsal, it's now time to perform.

The key to a great performance is to quite simply make your audience fall in love with you. Think about a musician you've seen or heard perform and love. Ask yourself why you love them. Chances are it is not because of how good they are but how they've communicated and connected with you. They give you a complete experience in how they have made you feel and this is what you want to do for your friends, family, clients, colleagues, customers, crowds, whoever your audience is. You want to connect with them. You want to create a complete experience with your performance in order to create your own happiness and help and inspire others.

i. Confidence

Before you can begin to be confident about what you have to do, you have to have confidence in yourself. I know from personal experience that this can be really hard, especially when you may lack self-confidence in your height, size, age, looks, appearance or in what people think and say about you; however, being confident in yourself really is key to honestly performing in life.

Despite being able to stand on a stage and perform as a musician to a live audience as well as developing my own business portfolio, I've struggled with a lot of these self-confidence issues and at times they have been stifling. As you now know, my greatest nemesis has been the words and actions of other people both to my face and behind my back and this, combined with the fact I've never been overly confident about my looks, size or appearance, has, on occasions, felt crippling.

I'd always put on a brave face, though, and crack on with what needed to be done, but ultimately, that course of action is not maintainable. Your confidence is knocked and your sparkle is dampened; your personal performance can't go on without its shining star.

So, what to do? Well, the only way to start getting your confidence intact is to start with yourself. Remember my friend I quoted as saying *other people's opinion of you is not your concern?* He was right. It took some thinking about, but ultimately it was these words and the support of my husband Simon that set me back on track to having self-confidence in what and who I am and what I do.

I often say you can't help people if they're not willing to help themselves, and this is true when it comes to gaining confidence. The thing is, in this situation, the person you're helping is yourself and there's little things you can do and changes you can make that will help you feel more confident in yourself.

Let's take a look at some of the things you can do to increase your confidence and control your nerves and anxiety, starting with a quick re-visit to the idea of diet and exercise. Simple things such as drinking water, eating well and a little exercise, as we discussed in Productivity, can have a great effect on how you feel. If I know I'm doing the best I can for me in this department, it certainly makes me feel and look better. I can notice the colour in my face and sparkle in my eyes. Likewise, making an effort to feel good in what I'm wearing gives me more confidence than just sat working in my pyjamas (don't get me wrong, I love pyjama days but when you work from home you can start to feel a little drained by the permanent pj status!).

What You Wear

If, like me, you've never been inclined to be a shopper or, like I've been most of my life, without the funds to consider clothes shopping a priority, when you do buy clothes for yourself, make sure that they make you feel good when you wear them and buy something you'll actually wear often. Investing in clothes that make you feel great is a win for your self-confidence and much better than buying an item for buying's sake. The clothes don't have to be expensive, but they do have to make you feel fabulous and full of confidence.

Smile

Cheaper than any clothes you could buy and guaranteed to make you feel better, boost your confidence and encourage a positive response from people is simply wearing a smile every day. When we genuinely smile or laugh, it lights up our faces, especially our eyes, and radiates a sunshine. Truly good and happy thoughts will make you feel better instantly, probably make you stand up a little straighter, make you feel more confident and put you in a fantastic mood.

If you have good thoughts, they will shine out of your face like sunbeams and you will always look lovely. Roald Dahl, author.

When I go for a walk – another of those activities that always makes me feel better and more confident – I make a point of smiling and saying hello to everyone I see. The response you get back is warm and friendly (though there may be a hint of surprise with some people!) and the interaction is a lovely boost to your mood and confidence. Go on, try it. Go for a walk and smile and say hello to everyone you pass and see how it makes you feel.

Positivity

To me, positivity does not mean things will turn out OK, but that you will be OK regardless of how things turn out. I choose to be positive every day. It's not just something that happens, it really is a choice; and it's a choice you could make, too. For me, the choice to be positive gives me confidence, because I have that belief and knowledge that no matter what happens, I will be OK. Whether it's making a business judgment to try something new in order to develop your services or finances or it is a choice at home as a parent, making a decision is much easier if you've chosen to be positive, because you have that safety net that regardless of what happens, everything will be OK. But you have to make a decision, whether it's personal or professional. Often, just that act of commitment can give you confidence because, in removing the doubt or what-ifs in your head, you will have removed the anxiety also.

My choice to be positive has definitely stood me in good stead when embracing grief and other issues, though it has come under criticism from certain people who foolishly believe they thrive off the negative (they're not thriving, they are in fact draining themselves professionally, personally and socially). I don't refer to it as 'dealing with' or 'getting over' grief, as many people do. I truly believe there is no getting over or dealing with losing someone you love. Since this will always be with me, my positivity has allowed me to embrace it. This means I'm kind to myself and know it's OK to be intensely sad at times, but also productive, happy and ambitious at exactly the same time. The emotions *can* co-exist.

My positivity also helped me care for Simon when he had cancer and spent three weeks in an induced coma in ICU. The positivity was never the ideal that life was going to go back to how it had been and everything was going to be great again: it was the knowledge I had, thanks to my choice to be positive, that whatever the outcome was going to be, life would go on regardless ... and it does. But most noticeably to me is how, despite the worst of things happening in my world, this practice of positivity has boosted my self-confidence immeasurably and for the first time, I genuinely feel OK about who I am.

You gain strength, courage, and confidence by every experience in which you really stop to look fear in the face. You are able to say to yourself, 'I lived through this horror. I can take the next thing that comes along.' Eleanor Roosevelt.

Mindfulness

Even now, in 2019, the mention of mindfulness sends some people thinking about chanting hippies living in communes. OK, maybe not that bad, but there is still a lack of understanding about mindfulness. Thankfully, a large movement of people are embracing it – I am one of those people. Simply put, mindfulness is the process of bringing your focus and awareness to the present moment.

How often have you gone over past scenarios in your head and relived moments that make you angry or upset? Or maybe you've had a whole conversation in your head with another person, pre-empting their responses and your reactions (usually only to find out the situation never actually goes as you imagined)? Yes, well I have, too, and all it's resulted in is me feeling upset, anxious, angry and obnoxious, or a whole host of other negative emotions, and having reduced self-confidence.

With the practice of mindfulness, when you feel yourself reflecting negatively or jumping ahead with your thoughts in this way, you draw your mind to the present moment. There are many ways to do this, from taking a few minutes to sit down, close your eyes and focus on your breathing to going for a walk, where you really take in the sights and sounds around you. This practice brings you back to the here and now, where you can be confident in yourself. It focusses your mind, allowing you to experience clarity, which will in turn lead you to communicate well.

Don't think you have to convert to some kind of meditation guru, though. Mindfulness can be practised in so many ways, from drawing to walking, from yoga to listening to music. Whatever your chosen medium, just focus on the right now.

When you're actually practising mindfulness and taking a moment with your thoughts, your mind will wander. You will think of things past and future, but that's OK. Don't beat yourself up about it: just acknowledge it and bring your thoughts back to the present. Practising mindfulness for just a few minutes can make a huge difference to your confidence levels.

Do not dwell in the past, do not dream of the future, concentrate the mind on the present moment. Buddha.

Be Kind to Yourself

You know those conversations in your head I just mentioned in Mindfulness, well how about the conversations you have in your head with yourself? The ones where you convince yourself you're not good enough, or don't look your best, or can't achieve something, or that good things only happen to other people. Sound familiar? I'm pretty sure those conversations are commonplace in many people's minds!

Ask yourself this: would you honestly say those things to someone else – a friend, family member, colleague or even a stranger? Would it be OK to say this to someone else or would you be worried about hurting their feelings? If not, then why would it be OK to hurt your own feelings with these negative conversations?

The answer: it's not. By having negative discussions with yourself, you are draining every last bit of confidence out of yourself. You're not being 'cruel to be kind' or 'real' or 'honest' with yourself, you're just being mean and tarnishing your sparkle.

Just be kind; to other people, yes, but most of all to yourself. Encourage and champion yourself, because if you don't, how can you expect other people to? A few kind words to yourself in your internal monologue can have a lasting impact on your confidence, so hush your inner critic.

Nerves

Right, this is a biggy. Nerves and anxiety play a huge part in all our lives and they can make us lose confidence in ourselves and everything we've ever worked for or done. But they don't have to.

Embrace your nerves. Yes, that's right, embrace them. The worst thing you can do is try to suppress your nerves and keep them down. It won't work. Accept them and bring them into your world by acknowledging them, rationalising them and using them as passionate inspiration to sound or be enthusiastic.

When someone tells me that they are nervous (common when I'm dealing with brides on their wedding day, musicians about to perform or someone about to embark on public speaking), I always explain to them that nerves and excitement give us the same physical sensations, therefore what you're feeling is more likely to be excitement than nerves and, as such, you can really look forward to what's about to happen.

You have to learn the difference between legitimate nerves and fear and unfounded anxiety. Something can feel really scary, such as public speaking or walking down the aisle, but in fact you're not in any danger, whereas finding yourself swimming in an ocean with sharks for company, that's real fear.

It's not the nerves or fear, but how you react to them that counts. You see, it's easy to *react* to things as opposed to *act*. We let our overall mood dictate our actions, consequently destroying our confidence and course of action.

Next time you think you feel nervous or anxious, try and break things down in your mind to ascertain whether it's legitimate nerves or unfounded anxiety, then take control of your emotions. Reframe your thoughts to make the situation positive and one you can find some enjoyment in.

Focus on your breathing. Control your breath to keep it natural. Breathe through your nose and out through your mouth. If you're having to speak, be sure to take breaths between sentences and slow yourself down. In fact, when preparing for a performance of any kind, slow everything down; take time to do your regular activities to keep your heart rate calm. Also, before you start, take 30 seconds to breathe with your eyes closed to really focus and centre yourself or get an app such as Calm, which has controlled breathing sessions.

Most importantly, remember you are in control of your mood, emotions and responses, so act and don't react. By gaining control, you will feel yourself fill with confidence and go on to give a great performance.

Power Pose

I have to touch on power poses. It's a bit controversial as to whether they are a real thing or not, but I say if it works for you, then go for it! The power pose, to quote Wikipedia, is *a controversial hypothesis in psychology that claims that by assuming a 'powerful' posture, subjects can induce positive hormonal and behavioural changes.*

Basically, it's standing assertively and authoritatively, like Wonder Woman or Superman with their hands on their hips. The best example of it I've seen is in the hit TV show Grey's Anatomy when the surgeons undertake a power pose prior to surgery. (Don't judge me for being a Grey's Anatomy fan!) If it makes you feel good though and gives you confidence, pose away!

Visualisation

Visualisation is a powerful technique and can help raise your confidence because, when used positively, you form a mental image of your success and achievements.

The best-selling book *The Secret,* by Rhonda Byrne, is based on the theory of the law of attraction, which claims that thoughts can change someone's life. Visualisation and manifestation can make amazing things happen. Some people really buy into this, whilst others are a little more sceptical. That aside, I think there are definitely some merits to using visualisation as a tool to focus on your success.

Visualisation is not just positive thinking or imagining you can do something, but a much deeper thought process where you can close your eyes and embrace all your senses in order to truly feel what it would be like to achieve your goals. I'm not an accomplished runner and so when I run the London Marathon in April 2019, I will be relying on the fitness of my mind to get me round the course. I know I'm going to successfully complete the challenge. Why? Because when I close my eyes I can see, feel and hear what it's going to be like running down The Mall after 26 miles; I can feel the pain in my legs and tears running down my face; and I can taste the glass of champagne I'm going to drink afterwards! I can feel how emotional the whole event is going to be, so much so I am having to fight back the tears now. Still, it makes me feel great and confident knowing I'm going to successfully undertake the marathon – and that's what visualisation can do, combined with a bit of physical training in my case. In recalling Benjamin Zander's giving yourself an A, if you visualise your A, you move from a place of possibility; and combined with productivity and a good strategy, you will gain confidence to give your best performance and achieve your success.

Visualisation is the process of creating pictures in your mind of yourself enjoying what you want. When you visualise, you generate powerful thoughts and feelings of having it now. The law of attraction then returns that reality to you, just as you saw it in your mind. Rhonda Byrne, author.

Learning

In order to gain confidence, one thing we can do is extend our comfort zone so that what we originally felt unconfident about achieving begins to fall well within our comfortable personal parameters. One of the best ways to extend your comfort zone is by learning.

We're not talking about giant leaps into the unknown here, rather taking small, incremental steps to develop your knowledge and, consequently, your comfort zone. I am a huge advocate of learning hence my comfort zone constantly shifts. One day I can be a musician and the next we're opening a catering division of our business, despite me not being a chef. (That happened after a conversation over a meal in Italy and then Café Umbria was born!)

I learn in many ways, particularly through reading – every variety of book and subject. What is equally important for learning is listening and talking to people. You can learn so much from everyone around you; everyone has a fascinating story or experience to tell if they're given an opportunity to share it. Ask questions. Questions will expose you to even more knowledge and, as they say, knowledge is power.

Work on constantly developing your skill set and embrace learning. Learning really doesn't stop when you leave school; that's when it starts. As you learn, your comfort zone will shift and in turn your confidence will blossom, allowing you to do more and to perform boldly and happily.

The Company You Keep

American entrepreneur and motivational speaker Jim Rohn is attributed as saying, *You are the average of the five people you spend the most time with.*

The company you choose to keep can have a huge impact on your life in terms of your mood, confidence levels and success. We can feel inspired or drained by people (I happen to like *mood hoovers* to describe social drainers), which is why it's important to choose your company wisely when trying to boost your confidence levels.

Think about your own social circles for a minute. Who are you spending the majority of your time with? Do they lift you up or drag you down? Being in the company of people who are high achievers is likely to help you achieve more. The company of great leaders (and I don't mean country leaders or heads of state, more friends, family or colleagues who have good leadership qualities) can inspire us to succeed, and associating with people who are happy and positive will more often than not encourage a happy and positive outlook of our own. The opposite is also true. *Mood hoovers* drag us down and deplete our confidence and energy levels.

Being a social butterfly or the go-to person for people is all well and good but not to the detriment of yourself. Select your social and business circles wisely so it serves you and increases your confidence and success. Know what you need and don't be shy of filling your life with people that share your goals and aspirations – people that elevate you.

If anyone in your life threatens your confidence, mental wellbeing or success, then remember to put your needs first and either address the issue or remove them from your life. All you need to focus on is you: your needs, desires, aspirations and wellbeing. Make yourself the priority and soon you will gravitate to all the right people in your life who will love and support you and share in your hopes and dreams.

Remember, it is all about you. Everything you do should be for the benefit of you, your confidence, your success and your happiness.

ii. Competence

In order to be competent, you must be confident in yourself and your skill set. In the words of American author Mary Jo Putney, *competence is a great creator of confidence.* The two work hand in hand, along with clarity and communication, to help you perform at your peak to reach your goals, no matter how big or small they are.

Competence is the ability to do something successfully and efficiently. It is not about other people's perception of your abilities, but your self-confidence in what and how you do things. Being competent is about being an authority in your field of expertise, whether that is getting your kids ready for school by 7am, running a multinational company, playing a Bach sonata from memory or securing A grades in all your assignments.

You don't have to be the best at what you do, you don't have to have been working in your field the longest, you don't have to be the most experienced or be working the longest hours, but what you must have is belief, confidence and the ability to communicate and engage with others. That is competence. If you have something to say, then say it. Your passion and beliefs are worth everything and will resonate with someone. Learn and develop all the time, be accepting of others' views and don't be following others – that is the key to competence.

Let's look at a few of the key elements to showing your competence.

Being an Expert

When you have confidence and have learned your trade within your personal or professional life, you can share your knowledge and experience with others. It's OK to have your say and speak up, to enable your story to inspire others. Being an expert does not mean you have to be the best, oldest or most experienced at what you do, but it does mean that your confidence, knowledge and skills combined allow you to be an authority in what and how you do things.

Share your knowledge and stories with others through the medium of writing blogs or books or creating podcasts or TV channels. There is such an array of social media platforms to share your worth on these days and build your audience. The more you share the more confident you will become and the more you will be seen as an authority. Start conversations on subjects that you're knowledgeable about and encourage people to join in. Never be afraid of your opinion or outlook on things.

Using social media to create groups for people who share your thoughts is a great way to share your story, and people will respect you for your expertise and competence. Being open, honest and helpful will inspire people to tackle challenges in their own lives. This is one of the humbling privileges about being competent and confident. But remember! Even when you're an expert, you must never stop learning.

Never become so much of an expert that you stop gaining expertise. View life as a continuous learning experience. Denis Waitley, motivational speaker.

Experience

An investment in knowledge pays the best interest. Benjamin Franklin, founding father of the USA.

Doing one thing over and over again in the same way does not make you experienced: it makes you good at doing one thing. Experience comes from learning and developing, extending your comfort zone and trying new things to broaden your horizons, making you more competent at what you do, especially if you try doing things in many different ways.

The best teachers are those that have actually experienced their area of expertise in many different real and physical ways, not those who have learned their trade just from a book. Reading and learning is vital to developing your knowledge, but you will never be truly competent in something until you fully experience it. Experience is the knowledge and skill you gain when you expose yourself to a certain thing, so the more you expose yourself to new things, the more experienced you will become.

I am a huge believer that life should be about experiences. In fact, I like to gift experiences as opposed to material things. Whether it's a massage or a ghost tour, afternoon tea at the Cat Café or a short trip, experiences are what open our eyes to the world and give us knowledge and more experience of what and how we do things.

There is no point sitting on your sofa wishing you could do things. Whether it's travel, learning to dance or starting your own business, get out there and do it. Know it's possible for you to try these things, put a plan in place, extend your comfort zone and grow your experience in order to be confident and competent in what you do, and enjoy all the experiences along the way.

Develop & Grow

Thrive from learning, enjoy it and embrace it.

Many young people can't wait to finish school because they have had enough of learning and want to escape the school system. It's a shame that they think learning only happens in the confines of school, because everything around us is a lesson – people, places and products.

If you open your eyes and mind to developing yourself and growing as a person, you soon realise life is one big lesson; and the biggest way in which we develop and grow is by trying and failing. But we are often scared: scared of getting things wrong and scared of failing.

When you first become a parent you think you have to be perfect, but how can you be? We've already established that perfection is a myth! You've never been a parent before, so you can't be expected to get everything right. What does happen is that we learn as we go and this develops and grows us as people.

If we always got everything right, we would never develop, we would never learn. Failure gives us an opportunity to learn from our mistakes and try things again differently. The experience of failing strengthens us and makes us develop. It makes us more competent in what we do because we have learned the biggest lesson: how not to do something.

So, don't be scared of failure. Take every opportunity to develop and grow and enjoy the lessons – the easy and the tough ones!

Strive to Be Your Best

Whether it's being a parent, completing your degree, running your own business or being a friend, don't focus too hard on being THE best and concentrate all your energies on being YOUR best. The only thing you should be interested in is waking up every day and being the best version of yourself. In the same way you created your to-do lists in the section on Productivity, each morning set out in your mind what you want to achieve and why, and, at the end of the day, ask yourself what worked and what could be done differently to develop yourself and be your best.

Remember: other people's opinions are not your concern, so focus on you only and what you need to do in order to achieve your goals and be your best self. Don't worry about what your peers or competitors may be doing or how they're doing things. Yes, be aware, but don't be infatuated with it.

You've set out your goals and developed your plan, now it's time to give your performance. You will rock it, whatever it is, as long as you have confidence and competence. Evolve yourself organically. By this I mean don't think you have to conform to other people's ideals or ways of doing things. This is your journey, your life, your goals. Do it your way at your speed and whatever you want to achieve, be your best at doing it.

Preparation

Any athlete, musician, teacher or academic will tell you that in order to both appear to be and actually be competent at what you do, you need to be prepared. Preparation is absolutely key to competence: if you don't know your stuff, you're really not going to fool anyone.

But – and here's the thing – yes, it is possible to fake it until you make it, but only up to a point. Faking it until you make it is when you imitate confidence and competence and use a positive mindset to become something different. You have to be doing it for the right reasons. If your plan is to make yourself appear better than you are or prove your worth to others, then the faking-it plan is more likely to backfire on you. But if you know there's something inside you holding you back from achieving your goals, then faking it and pretending to be the person you want to be could well be the trigger to help you change the way you think and feel. Whilst I've successfully used this tactic, it's no substitute for doing your homework and being truly prepared. It doesn't always work.

To help you perform your best when you need to, preparation is essential. There are some simple preparation habits you can develop. Do you know what they are? All the things I discuss in this book! Mentally and physically prepare yourself to achieve your goals and do the work to strengthen yourself. I like this concept: *Get fit to do sport, don't do sport to get fit*. Do all the necessary preparation to get yourself match-fit. To stick with the sports analogies, if you wanted to get really good at doing sit-ups, you wouldn't just do sit-ups, you'd strengthen all your core body muscles in order to be your best.

Apply this to your preparation. Don't just prepare the one thing you want to achieve: look at the wider plan that you can prepare in order to be confident, competent and to perform at your peak.

Practice

Practice, practice, practice. As dull as it sounds (and yes, we've all witnessed the child that doesn't want to do their piano practice because it's boring!), after preparation, practice is the only thing that's going to give you a sparkling and polished performance. Practice is not just about doing something repetitively, though: it's about preparing yourself for every scenario so you know what could go right or wrong and how you would then deal with it.

Practice will help you master your skill and it can be relevant to a wide range of goals, from learning a language to public speaking. We've covered many of the skills to help you practise in the most productive way, such as limiting distractions and visualising. Practising allows you to focus on your quality and to make sure you are prepared for every eventuality. Similar to when I discussed failure, getting things wrong when you practise is good as the likelihood is you won't make the same mistake twice.

Break things down into small chunks so you can really focus on certain aspects and then apply them to a bigger picture. Maybe you're learning Italian for your forthcoming holiday. Start with a few basic words, then put those into a sentence that will help you pay for a bill. When you're on your holiday, make a point of going into three shops consecutively and using the phrase. Having practised it, and visualised yourself doing it, it'll be secured in your head and will become easy to use with confidence and competence.

So, break things down, small bitesize bits first, then build up your practice. Work on the theory of three: practise three things consecutively and correctly to confirm it in your mind and you'll be ready to perform in a natural and relaxed manner.

iii. Clarity

How can we get clarity? The best way is by having total understanding and confidence in ourselves and our message. Understanding ourselves is vital because it means we are aware of our emotions and feelings and we know how we may react and can act in situations, such as feeling nervous or anxious. If we have clarity on this, then we can embrace these feelings rather than trying to suppress them. That is one of the most important factors when mastering our skills and controlling nerves.

In order to understand yourself and increase your self-confidence, you need to consider the following:

Your Brand

Your brand is the most valuable asset you have, but the mistake so many people make is thinking a brand is just relative to a business. It's not. We each have our personal brand, too: our identity. Whether we're talking about you as an individual or a business, your brand is everything about you, a reflection of your personality, ethos, mission and so much more. It is your smile, the colours you use, the clothes you wear, the words you speak and the correspondence you send.

Your brand is you, so be honest about who you are and true to yourself in order to really express it.

Ask yourself the following questions to understand your brand:

- What do you stand for?
- What are your beliefs?
- What is your heart and soul?

When you've got these answers, you can begin to understand your own personal brand and can apply that to what and how you do things. It will become part of your overall performance.

Your Story

What's your story – your real, core, honest story – and how does this relate to what you want people to know? Have you ever sat down and written about yourself, asking yourself who you are and where you come from? Possibly not, but if you came face to face with a branding expert or therapist, they'd ask you all reams of questions about your past. Your past may not seem relevant to an issue or task in hand in the present day, but our stories are what have led us to the place we are now. Our stories have shaped and moulded us into the people we are. The good, the bad and the downright ugly all play pivotal roles in our lives and in order to gain clarity in your own head and in the way you communicate and perform, you need to have a full understanding and acceptance of your own story.

Why not write the story of your life? It could make for interesting reading.

Be an advocate for the people and causes important to you, using the most powerful tool only you have – your personal stories. John Capecci and Timothy Cage, authors.

Make it Personal

Don't be afraid to get personal about yourself. You might think people won't find you interesting or you don't have a story to tell, but everyone has a personal story which will resonate with and inspire someone. Don't be shy about it. Your personal experiences and honesty could be the refreshing words that give someone clarity about their own situation.

Being honest with yourself about your own story will solidify your thoughts to help you succeed. If you're being honest and personal, then you are working from a place of emotional meaning, which will help you give your finest performance in life and business.

A Clear Message

Now you have your own brand and story in place and you are being candid, ask yourself what is your message and who is your audience. One way to gain clarity about your message is to try the following simple exercise:

Tell me your personal or business message in no more than two sentences.

For example, for my new wedding planning business, my message aimed at keeping brides calm and relaxed as they plan their wedding could be: 'For stress-free wedding chat, planning, design and management, The Calm Bride from Mode for... Events is the complete wedding specialist. They create a completely relaxed client experience and know what clients think, want and how they want to feel.'

A clear message is a great asset in business and your personal life. At home, you may want to portray to your children the benefits of not spending so much time on computers, phones and on social media (good luck with that one!). Explain in two sentences why you don't believe it's healthy or appropriate. This is your message that you can clearly and consistently articulate (the kids will love that!).

Elevator pitches are also a good format on which to mould your story, a short description delivered in a way that anyone can understand in a short space of time. Don't overcomplicate what you want to say.

Written v Spoken

Delivering your message in either written or spoken format abides by the same rules. Make it sharp, consistent and deliver it with confidence. Don't use ten words if one will suffice. People have short attention spans; it's not just goldfish! And remember: body language is hugely important, and silence speaks volumes!

Your Audience

It's all very well understanding your own story, but what audience are you performing to? Is it your family at home, friends in the pub, colleagues at work or a room full of strangers? You want to be delivering your message to the right people. Find your people; people who are interested in you and what you have to say. Don't waste your time and energy on those who are not interested in supporting you. When you find your real audience (it may be prospective business clients or a group of friends), it will give you instant confidence and clarity and you will feel relaxed and energised because you will have their support. Whether you're in the pub on a Friday night or performing on stage to a concert hall of thousands, performing feels so much easier when you have the knowledge that everyone listening to you is on your side and willing you to be amazing.

Most of all, understand that not everyone is going to be in your fan club – and that is OK. I spent years thinking I had to please everyone; I was a habitual people pleaser. The best lesson I learned was that I didn't have to please any of them. The only person I had to please was myself. What a relief that lesson was to learn.

Be Social ... and Sociable

Don't be a hermit and hide away. Embrace people, whether it's via social media platforms or by going out to meet new people in any social setting.

Whilst people can break you (learned that one first-hand), they can also empower you – but only if you let them. Be social and sociable: don't just interact with the same people. They may feel safe, but it won't help you grow and I want you to grow like the blooming flower you really are. Meet new and exciting characters and learn from them. Meet people who challenge you and inspire you. Meet the people who will give the clarity YOU deserve and want.

iv. Communication

As human beings, we are designed to tell stories; it's been part of our evolution and history for thousands of years, but despite this natural 'in-built' skill, many people still find the art of relaying their story one of the most frightening and difficult challenges to face.

Communication does not come easily to some people and that can be for a variety of reasons. From nerves to feeling inadequate, from not knowing what to say to being overbearing, the art of communication is a skill that we all need to develop to be understood.

Whatever and however you are communicating, remember you don't need to be perfect. You need to be clear and concise but most of all you need to be natural, so don't shy away from it. The rules are the same regardless of how you communicate. You may be speaking in private or in public, you might be singing or dancing, performing on stage or grappling with a toddler. Every situation requires us to communicate with ease and fluidity.

But how can I be natural when I'm scared stiff? I hear you crying. Simple. Let's break it down, using public speaking as an example; after all, we all encounter some form of public speaking in our lives, whether it is to an audience of one or one thousand. Public speaking is a skill nearly everyone can adopt, just like walking, eating and riding a bike. You can train yourself in the key strengths, which we know are: clarity, confidence, competence and communication.

To communicate, you must be understandable and make your audience fall in love with you. As a performing musician, I tried to tell a musical story every time I played. My story was not better, but it was different to another musician's story. We all have a different understanding and view but my performance connected with 'my' audience and that was the only audience I

118

was interested in. Your own audience will respect you and believe in your passion. Work hard to connect and find your audience, not someone else's. But remember, your audience will change over the years as you develop and learn.

Once we have these four key strengths under our belts, we can then focus on the taboo of controlling our nerves and emotions, which we have already discussed. Do you feel nervous or flustered when trying to communicate with people? Remember what I said earlier about embracing and being aware of emotions. This will serve you much better than trying to suppress or hide them. Everyone gets nervous, but the key is how we control those nerves.

Here's a quick reminder of a few tips on how to combat nerves:

- Slow things down.
- Breathe deeply and slowly, controlling the breath to lower the heart rate.
- Prepare and practise your delivery.

You should now possess the power of confidence and clarity, your brand, your message, the right audience and also feel truly competent thanks to extending your comfort zone. You have everything in place to communicate and that's all you need to do now.

Your performance is ready, you've done the work and are fully prepped and rehearsed. This is why this section on communication can be the shortest, because everything we have discussed has led us, fully prepared, to this point.

As they say in the military: *Train hard, fight easy.*

It's time for the performance of your life! Break a leg!

10

Conclusion

If you have read this book up to this point, you will have gone through all the skill sets required to perform, whatever your chosen performance field. We have looked at believing things are possible, how to be productive and make a plan and how to give an honest and relaxed performance.

The Three Ps is my method of balancing everything life throws at me with happiness. When you've adopted the ways of The Three Ps, happiness will blossom, regardless of any difficulties or sadness you have to face.

Why? Because happiness is a choice and because it is an emotion that can co-exist with others. It is not a polar opposite to sadness. By utilising the methods of The Three Ps, you have got your life in check and made a habit of the skills which will get you through everything you need to do, whether that's running a successful household of one or a multinational company. That means you can focus on being happy and enjoying the things in life you want to. That positivity you've now acquired – the knowledge that you will be OK regardless of what happens in life – has led you to believe the things you want in life are possible, that you can be productive and that you don't have to fear performing.

You've got all the knowledge inside you now, so grow, learn, develop, share your story, inspire, be bold, be brave, be sad, be kind, be successful, be awesome, be passionate, be confident, be competent, but, most of all, never stop learning and choose to be … happy.

The time has come for you to *#createmyhappy*. Enjoy every moment and experience.

Much love and thanks for reading my story.

Tabby xxx

11

Recommended Reading List

I have hundreds of favourite books, but these are just a few of the ones which have truly inspired me and which I've referred to in this book.

Eat That Frog!	Brian Tracy
Fish	Stephen C. Lundin, Harry Paul and John Christensen
How To Be F*cking Awesome	Dan Meredith
Leave Your Mark	Aliza Licht
S.U.M.O.	Paul McGee
The Art of Brilliance	Andy Cope and Andy Whittaker
The Art of Possibility	Rosamund and Benjamin Zander
The Chimp Paradox	Professor Steve Peters
The Secret	Rhonda Byrne

Printed in Great Britain
by Amazon